The Monastic Way

The Monastic Way

Edited by

Hannah Ward and Jennifer Wild

WILLIAM B. EERDMANS PUBLISHING COMPANY
GRAND RAPIDS, MICHIGAN / CAMBRIDGE, U.K.

First published 2006 in the United Kingdom by
the Canterbury Press Norwich
(a publishing imprint of Hymns Ancient & Modern Limited,
a registered charity)
9–17 St Alban's Place, London
NI ONX
www.scm-canterburypress.co.uk
and in 2007 in the United States of America by
Wm. B. Eerdmans Publishing Company
2140 Oak Industrial Drive NE, Grand Rapids, Michigan 49505 /
P.O. Box 163, Cambridge CB3 9PU U.K.
www.eerdmans.com

Printed and bound in Great Britain by William Clowes Ltd, Beccles, Suffolk

10 09 08 07   5 4 3 2 1

ISBN 978-0-8028-4045-5

The editors and publisher acknowledge with thanks permission to
quote from *The Sayings of the Desert Fathers: The Alphabetical
Collection*, trans. Benedicta Ward SLG, Cistercian Publications/
A.R. Mowbray, 1984. Reproduced by kind permission of
Continuum International Publishing Group.

Contents

Abbreviations of names of monastic orders   vi

Introduction   vii

List of illustrations   xii

January   *Starting out*   1

February   *Seeking guidance*   19

March   *Living with others*   35

April   *Going to work*   53

May   *Balancing life*   69

June   *Talking money*   87

July   *Learning to listen*   103

August   *Working for justice*   123

September   *Opening our eyes*   141

October   *Saving the planet*   159

November   *Giving and receiving*   177

December   *Endings and beginnings*   195

List of sources   215

Biographical index   236

Abbreviations of names of monastic orders

cscl	Community of St Clare, Freeland, Oxfordshire (who now use osc)
o carm	Carmelite Order
o cart	Carthusian Order
OCD	Discalced Carmelite Order
o cist	Cistercian Order
OCSO	Order of Cistercians of the Strict Observance
OSB cam	Camaldolese Benedictine
OSB	Order of St Benedict
OSC	Order of St Clare

Introduction

The words monastery and monk, convent and nun, have been heard rather more widely than usual recently, especially in the UK, heralding and following two television series that have perhaps surprised even their makers by the interest they have generated. Not only have viewers been given a chance to see behind the closed doors of monastery or convent and watch the monks or nuns as they go about their daily routine – they've also been able to follow to some extent the experiences of the groups of 'ordinary' people who were allowed to spend forty days and forty nights, a limited but substantial period, living alongside the monks or nuns, learning about their way of life by sharing it and at the same time exploring their own reactions to it.

Many, if not most, people will have known in any case that Christian monks and nuns exist, and perhaps that the monastic life has been around for some time (think of those romantic ruins scattered round Britain – Fountains Abbey, Glastonbury Abbey, Tintern Abbey and so on). In fact it all began long before those monasteries were built. Into the deserts of Egypt and other countries round the eastern end of the Mediterranean, in the third and fourth centuries, came some individual men and women, intent on fighting their way to holiness and God, as they saw it, by going away from their fellows to confront the evil in themselves and the world, and to take their part in the struggle for the purity of heart without which the Kingdom of God cannot be finally established in God's world. We are lucky that the many anecdotes told of and by these often amazing, or eccentric or sometimes just odd individuals were collected up by various disciples or serious-minded

visitors who wanted to preserve their wisdom in writing. The sayings of these abbas and ammas, the Desert Fathers and Mothers,
are quite often quoted in the pages of this book, along with tales
about them and their doings. They often make more entertaining
and edifying reading than much of what has been written since
by their successors. Perhaps brevity is the soul of wisdom as well
as of wit?

Gradually groups of hermits began to gather together and so the
seeds of monasticism were sown. The oldest occupied Christian
monastery, that of St Antony, in the Eastern Desert of Egypt,
founded soon after the death of Antony himself in 356, and apparently near to the place where he had spent many years in solitude
before emerging to join those who wanted to be his disciples, is
still flourishing and is occupied by monks of the Egyptian Coptic
Church. (For some views of the monastery and its surroundings
see http://www.egyptmyway.com/photo/st_antony1_1html.)

In the 1,650 years since Antony's time monasticism has travelled far, both in geographical and in cultural terms, and in a very
great variety of practice. The Orthodox Churches (definitively
separated from the Latin Church of the West in the eleventh century) have their own long history of later developments in monastic life, the 'Holy Mountain' (Mt Athos in northern Greece)
being perhaps the best-known cluster of monasteries. In the Latin
West Benedict had already written his Rule, in part a revised and
improved version of earlier attempts by others, and one that became the foundation document for Western monasticism. It has
since given rise to several 'reforms' and variations, all following
Benedict's Rule in their own ways.

We can only hint at the long and complex story of Christian
monasticism, but taking our cue from the word itself, we have
confined our choices in this collection to the writings of a few of
those monastics (male and female) whose lives have been based
on the ideal of 'stability' – they have tended to stay put, though in
remarkably varied degrees of seclusion, it is true. In the Western
Church it is particularly noticeable that in different countries and
continents monastics may look anything but 'enclosed'; many
Benedictine abbeys in Europe, for instance, founded monasteries

in North America in response to the call to educate the children of Catholic immigrants there, while their European counterparts were more likely to remain without much or any active involvement in the world outside the monastery. We have included extracts from the writings of some Poor Clares and Carmelite nuns, not technically described as monastic, but (in some parts of the world) more strictly 'stay-at-home' than most male Benedictines, let alone Franciscan or Carmelite friars, have ever been.

One might think that those men and women who join religious orders in the churches where their commitment to a life of service directly offered to those outside their religious house, teaching, nursing, running parishes and the like, would have more to say to the rest of us in our present-day world than the monk or nun whose base and workplace is essentially their monastery or convent itself. However, the simplicity and directness of a mature group of monastic men or women can sometimes listen and speak from a very down-to-earth experience of ordinary human life together, its struggles and its possibilities.

In compiling this collection we have chosen to use, as 'pegs' for each month's worth of extracts, activities or aspects of daily life that are familiar to all of us. In other words we, the monastic guests, are starting from where *we* are. And rather than trying to present monastic wisdom as snippets of good advice from them to us, we have aimed, as far as possible, to overhear monastics talking to each other – often, indeed, instructing or advising each other, but also often simply comparing notes. Either way we hope that this collection comes across as a conversation among equals, without any patronising element. It is true that sometimes in the past monastics could feel assured that theirs was the higher path, and others were content to have them speak as it were from another world. In the present age they have been learning fast, but we too have much to learn, and sometimes we can fruitfully listen to them, whether they are speaking to us or to each other.

The quotations at the head of each month, in some way illustrating the 'theme' of that month, are taken from two of the greatest Christian monastic rules. That of Benedict, as we have said, has been enormously influential in Western Europe and in all parts of the world affected by its religion and culture. Today its influence outside the monastic circle may be greater than ever, as many find its sober and moderate tone attractive and its wisdom a sound guide. The Rules written by Basil the Great crowned (for the Eastern part of the early Church) the efforts of the early abbas and ammas to learn how to live their lives in community, as this form of monastic living gradually overtook the hermit life. As Basil famously said, 'If you live alone, whose feet will you wash?' – and it might be observed that this intensely practical awareness of the implications of the gospel ('Good News') announced by Jesus can give rise to the current concern of many present-day monastics (among others) for issues of justice and peace, of human obligations to the well-being of this planet and all that is on and around it, and to sustained attempts to understand and relate to those of other faiths, particularly the monastics among them. Indeed, some of the quotations in this collection that relate to interfaith dialogue indicate the way in which aspects or forms of monastic spirituality cross boundaries of religion.

Though the extracts that follow are arranged in months they do not relate in any way to the usual markers of the Christian year, or to the seasons. (The fact that we tried not to put totally inappropriate readings on 25 and 31 December only reflects the current mood of our culture.) We hope the reader will feel free to start anywhere, and not necessarily treat this as simply a collection of daily readings, much less a collection that progresses from beginning to end as to some ultimate goal. These excerpts are offered as chances to listen to monastics, not necessarily to agree with them, but to hear at least some of their concerns and practices that resonate with our own desires and needs. The choice of passages is our own, and inevitably leaves out many great and beloved friends and mentors. (Another year?) But it seemed better to line up the relatively obscure alongside some of the well-known, and canonized saints alongside those who are never likely to come to the attention of earthly church authorities.

Sources of all the extracts are given in date order at the end of the book, and the Biographical Index gives a brief indication of the place and particular monastic way of the writers, and lists dates of all entries from their writings in this book. Those who have no date(s) supplied are assumed to be still alive.

Finally, our present age seems to be a remarkably introspective one. Religion can lend itself to this preoccupation, for good and for ill. Certainly 'the unexamined life is not worth living', as Socrates said, and some of the most shrewd and intelligent observers of the human spirit have been monastics; but in our search for passages that would say something to readers now, we have tried to concentrate on monasticism as illustrating a very human way of life, rather than as an interior journey par excellence.

A postscript: monastic writers can display a well-developed sense of humour. You may have to imagine the smile in the eyes of the speaker, at times.

List of illustrations

January
Glendalough Monastery at Annamoe, Co Wicklow, Ireland, founded by St Kevin, in the 6th century.

February
Quarr Abbey on the Isle of Wight, UK, founded in 1132 by Baldwin de Redvers, fourth Lord of the Isle of Wight.

March
The monastic complex founded in about the 7th century on the steep sides of the rocky island of Skellig Michael off the south west coast of Ireland.

April
Hand carving holding crosses at the Little Brothers of Francis Hermitage at Tabulam, New South Wales, Australia.

May
Novices at Santa Catalina Monastery at Arequipa, Peru, founded in about 1580.

June
Benedictine medal.

July
Reading the Rule of St Benedict.

August
Anti-war protest in Bethlehem.

September
Church window designed by Bronislaw Bak at St John's Abbey, Collegeville, Minnesota, USA.

October
Resurrection window by Tracey Sheppard for the Sisters of Bethany, Southsea, UK.

November
Fifth-century mosaic of loaves and fishes on the floor of an ancient church and monastery at Tabgha on the north shore of the Sea of Galilee.

December
Medieval painting of a tau cross.

January

Starting out

Let's make a start, then, late as it is, for the words of Scripture are calling us to get up: 'it is now the moment for you to wake out of sleep' (Romans 13.11).

Rule of Benedict, Prologue

I

Listen. Benedict deliberately chose this word as the beginning of his Rule. It also is the first word that strikes us when the Rule is read on January 1; and it stands as a kind of theme for every year. Benedict starts without preliminaries and addresses the person directly. The last word of this sentence forms an inclusion together with the first word: 'Listen – fulfil!' The entire verse describes this listening in its fullest sense.

... At the very beginning of the Rule, the person is confronted by a call, ultimately by the word of God. 'God spoke, and it came into being' (Genesis 1, cf. John 1.1). The word of God addresses us. The life of every person is a special realization of a personal divine call. The person is shown as someone whose essence it is to be called. This is our dignity and also our obligation.

Aquinata Böckmann OSB

2

One of the challenges of my life was a book of answers. And I once got into trouble for saying that some of the best heresies that I know are in that book, the Baltimore Catechism. Well, maybe they are not really heresies, but in some ways they are more pernicious.

One of the answers found there is: How did God make me? And the answer: God made me out of nothing. Isn't that a shocking thing for a child to hear? If you are made out of nothing, what are you worth? No, God did not make us out of nothing. And he did not make us out of something. But at every moment God brings us forth in his creative love, sharing with us something of his own divine being, goodness and life. That is how much we are loved. We are loved into being.

Basil Pennington OCSO

3

Encountering the Rule of Benedict during my initial formation years, I experienced life and possibility, challenge, dismay, and anger. While I was able to glean life-giving wisdom, I was consistently concerned with the voice and life experiences *not* found in Benedict's Rule and its interpretation. Writings that I encountered tended to presume a universal inclusivity of experience that was actually the experience of very few. Rarely were these writings critical or questioning of Benedict's Rule. I found that I was constantly translating and reinterpreting sections of the Rule to fit my own self-understanding and life experience.

Laura Swan OSB

4

As for me, what am I doing in this out-of-the-way place? I am ashamed to write it down. I have indeed abandoned my city life as being the cause of innumerable ills, but I cannot yet abandon my self. I'm like an inexperienced ocean-traveller, seasick and miserable, who is vexed because he thinks it is the great size of the vessel that is producing the considerable swell, and yet if he transfers to a lifeboat or dinghy he is still miserable and seasick. The wretched nausea simply changes vessels along with him. My experience is rather like this: I carry my inner problems around with me and so get no great benefit from this remote place.

Basil the Great

5

Abba Poemen said about Abba Pior that every single day he made a fresh beginning.

Abba Poemen

6

Finally ... we must love the age we live in. It should be evident that from the point of view of faith the best age for each of us is the one in which God has placed us, the one he has given us and we must give back to him, the one in which we can give ourselves to him. It's a great thing to be alive! A great grace simply to exist! God has chosen our age for us: this age that we receive from him and that is ours is the only age we have at our disposal. We have no right to prefer another one ... If we compare our age with those of the past, so far as we know them, ours is not the worst of them all, or even worse than many of them; it is better than many, and perhaps better than all of them. A positive point of view is the primary condition for making it better still.

Jean Leclercq OSB

7

I found myself without anything left. I had gotten to where I wanted to be, and my major question was 'So what?' I felt soulless. I was driven, but what had it gotten me? I couldn't sit still, And I certainly did not want to be with myself. But where did I start? I needed some inspiration. But I wasn't even listening. I was running. I was actually fleeing from myself.

I started my sabbatical with the feeling I had been shafted. Hoodwinked into joining a programme that propertied to be a training ground for formation leaders, and here it was saying

things like 'You have to start with yourself'. I was hurt. I was
a victim. But then I sat down and tried to take part in the programme. Then one day Sr Cecilia Goodman came and talked to
us. She told us about the Aborigines in Australia who do a walk-
about, actually a runabout. Running and running until exhausted
by the run, they fall to the ground in order to let their souls catch
up to them. It hit me right between the eyes. It catapulted down
into my very being. I recognised myself. I was sitting waiting for
my soul to catch up to me. It was a revelation.

Benedict Auer OSB

8

In order to pray more and better we must often do less, let go of
more things, give up numerous good intentions, and be content
to yield to the inner pressure of the Spirit the moment [the Spirit]
bubbles up in us and tries to win us over and take us in tow.
Ultimately all our attempts at prayer and all our methods must
come to a dead end and wither away in order that the Spirit of
Jesus may facilitate and validate his own prayer in our heart.

André Louf OCSO

9

Modern society has the idea that if you want to live a truly spiritual life, you have to leave life as we know it and go away by yourself and 'contemplate,' and that if you do, you will get holy. It is
a fascinating although misleading thought. The Rule of Benedict
says that if you want to be holy, stay where you are in the human
community and learn from it. Learn patience. Learn wisdom.
Learn unselfishness. Learn love. Then, if you want to go away
from it all, then and only then will you be ready to do it alone.
   There is, of course, an anchorite lurking in each of us who

wants to get away from it all, who finds the task of dailiness dev-
astating, who looks for God in clouds and candlelight ... [Bene-
dict] himself set out to live the spiritual life as a hermit and then
discovered, apparently, that living life alone is nowhere near as
searing of our souls as living it with others. It is one thing to plan
my own day well with all its balance and its quiet and its contemplative exercises. It is entirely another rank of holiness to let my
children and my superiors and my elderly parents and the needs
of the poor do it for me.

Joan Chittister OSB

10

The false self is deeply entrenched. You can change your name and
address, religion, country, and clothes. But as long as you don't
ask *it* to change, the false self simply adjusts to the new environment. For example, instead of drinking your friends under the
table, as a significant sign of self-worth and esteem, if you enter a
monastery, as I did, *fasting* the other monks under the table could
become your new path to glory. In that case, what would have
changed? Nothing.

Thomas Keating OCSO

11

The word 'searching' is very much a monk's word and recalls that
the raison d'être of every monastic vocation is 'to seek God', as
the Rule of St Benedict says. I am in search. I am trying to understand the ultimate purpose of my life, the meaning of it, and the
meaning of everything and everybody else. I want to know why I
am here and what I am for. It would be hard to establish answers
to these questions by a survey of public opinion. We are, as a society, confused, distracted, uninterested, in fact lost. But the idea

of searching can be stood on its head. It helps if we switch from the notion of our searching for God and instead think about God coming to find us, for after all that is the way it is. It is we who are lost. It is God who is looking for us.

Basil Hume OSB

12

If you want to ask the question, 'Am I making progress?' do not look at your meditation. There is only one way we can judge our progress and that is by the quality of our love.

As the mantra leads us ever further from self-centredness we turn more generously to others and receive their support in return. Indeed, our love for others is the only truly Christian way of measuring our progress on the pilgrimage of prayer.

John Main OSB

13

Sit in your cell as in paradise. Put the whole world behind you and forget it. Watch your thoughts like a good fisherman watching for fish. The path you must follow is in the Psalms – never leave it. If you have just come to the monastery, and in spite of your good will you cannot accomplish what you want, then take every opportunity you can to sing the Psalms in your heart and to understand them with your mind. And if your mind wanders as you read, do not give up; hurry back and apply your mind to the words once more. Realize above all that you are in God's presence, and stand there with the attitude of one who stands before the emperor. Empty yourself completely and sit waiting, content with the grace of God, like the chick who tastes nothing and eats nothing but what his mother brings him.

Romuald of Ravenna

14

We must not be slaves either of time or health; we cannot dispose of either as we will! If we thought of acting only when all the conditions were favourable, we would pass our lives doing nothing; or at least we would get out of life very little of what it can give us.

Go ahead! That is a phrase I like so much. Even if everything is far from perfect, we must learn to say it. And things will go ahead, since joy does not come from without or from circumstances. Its principal source is within us.

A Carthusian

15

We see that we cannot partake deeply of the life of God unless we change profoundly. It is therefore essential that we should go to God in order that he should transform and change us, and that is why, to begin with, we should ask for conversion.

Conversion in Latin means a turn, a change in the direction of things ... Conversion means that instead of spending our lives in looking in all directions, we should follow one direction only. It is turning away from a great many things which we value solely because they were pleasant or expedient for us. The first impact of conversion is to modify our sense of values. God being at the centre of all, everything acquires a new position and a new depth. All that is God's, all that belongs to him, is positive and real.

Anthony Bloom

16

The monastic journey is a special kind of life with its own set of difficulties. For one thing, it puts human relationships under a microscope. Although the trials are not as big as those outside the monastery, they may be more humiliating. Monastics get upset by trifles and can't even claim a good reason for feeling that way ...

A couple of years ago, I gave a conference to an assembly of lay organizations. These included marriage-encounter and social action groups, secular institutes, and new communities. My talk was based on monastic spirituality, but instead of saying 'monastic', I said 'Christian'. I was amazed to see how most people identified with this traditional teaching. It corresponded to their own experience. This reinforced my conviction that the spiritual journey is for every Christian who takes the Gospel seriously.

Thomas Keating OCSO

17

So why would I choose to live an enclosed, contemplative, monastic lifestyle? Because this is where I believe I can best give myself to others and because, most simply, this is where I believe I am being personally invited to live out my baptismal covenant. In the final analysis, I believe that we do not choose enclosure so much as discern whether it is a place we can find the intimacy we are called to and seek. By the sacramental reality of baptism, we are each called to holiness, to intimacy with God, and therefore we each need a special place in our lives where we can look after that relationship. This is mine. What is yours?

Jean Chively OSC

18

There is such widespread misunderstanding about the 'contemplative life' – the very phrase carries with it so many unconscious associations. To many it summons up a picture of lifeless people sitting around all day with little or nothing to do. But real prayer, coming from the silent center of our spirit, is the source of the selflessness of love, the source of energy. In that center, the source of our Being, we encounter God ... To find God is to find love. To find love is to find oneself in harmony with the basic energy of all creation, which is love. When a community is directed to this as its essential priority, ordinary limitations imposed on human relations by egoism become, as it were, flipped around. Where there was self-seeking there becomes service. Where there was desire for self-protection there becomes an impulse to lead others to fulfillment through love.

John Main OSB

19

Learning to surrender has its own cheap counterfeits. Passivity it is not, nor is it clenched-teeth conformity. Authentic self-gift requires freedom's consent and leads to growth in freedom. Strain is its antithesis. When individuals try too hard, when they attempt to do more than they can, they become exhausted, anxious, or chronically irritated. What should free them enslaves them. Formation becomes deforming.

Mari Beha OSC

20

Traditional teachings on the virtue of humility arose out of the experiences of men ... A woman's journey into humility has different nuances. There are two specific issues that need to be addressed in a woman's journey toward humility: a woman's sense of self and her relationship to power.

Women cannot give up a self they do not possess. A woman's journey into humility begins by discovering that she has a self and who this self is. Then she must struggle to live from this self. As natural connectors and builders of community, women make this journey as a *self-in-relation* ... This self-in-relation recognizes the importance of human community for our survival, as well as our happiness. Self-in-relation requires that we have a self to bring to community, and it acknowledges that we know ourselves because of our relationships with others.

Laura Swan OSB

21

The motives which lead young persons to knock on the door of the monastery are many. Good enough to justify the attempt, they are probably not adequate to keep them in the monastery all their lives. Most motivation needs to be examined in depth. The real motive lies beneath the surface and this must be brought to light. Only in this way will the determination to follow Christ in the monastic life be strengthened and at the same time the real meaning of the monastic life made clear. Whatever the motive that leads a young person to enter the monastery, a vocation is always an invitation which comes from God and not primarily from within oneself.

André Louf OCSO

22

In many ways, the concept of stability is the root vow for monastic identity. It contains two distinct elements, the first of which is commitment. A monk is committed not to an institution, nor to an ideal, nor to a philosophy or even to the Rule itself. The monk is committed to a community, to a group of people with its own particular past and present and future. Very often, this group of people is tied to a particular place, but it need not be so. Monks have always moved around, and no monastery can ever afford to put its physical location before its community. So what stability does is anchor the monk within a community, for better or for worse.

Timothy Wright OSB

23

Neither stability nor obedience could make sense without the third promise, that of conversion of life. It is always a danger that religious vows become static, that they describe things that either are, or more realistically are not. The call to conversion of life is in effect a vow to change, to never remain still either in self-satisfied fulfilment or in self-denying despair. There is no room for the person who thinks they have got it all sorted out, nor for the temptation in so many to believe that we will never even get started. It is a vow to believe in the possibility of change in ourselves, and also in others.

Timothy Wright OSB

24

Cranky elder. Sober judge. Austere administrator. Small wonder we often think of (and relate to) God with these images in mind. For these are *adult* images, and religion often seems designed for – and by – adults.

Adults may view Creator, creation, and creatures in such ways, but children interpret and relate to the world differently. The adult world runs on logic and efficiency, plans and procedures. The world of the child, however, is one of constant discovery: of give and take, of hide-and-seek. Adults demand that their God 'act like an adult': controlled, proper, antiseptic. But a child's God is friendly and fun: someone you can talk to, someone you can get dirty with.

Which view of God is correct? ... Perhaps occasionally we should imagine God shedding the black robes of the lawgiver and slipping into the bright play-clothes of a child. *For when asking who God is and how God 'works' in our lives, children are not the only ones who must learn and adults are not the only ones who can teach.*

Kurt Stasiak OSB

25

A discarded bottle lying on the ocean bottom is, it seems, an irresistible temptation for a baby crab. The little creature ... glides easily through the bottle's mouth to discover an enclosed world that offers everything it needs: plenty of organic debris to eat, shelter from strong currents, and, best of all, protection from the countless predators who feed on young crabs. Delighted, it makes itself at home, and begins to thrive in the cosy surroundings. After some weeks, however, when instinct tells it the time has come to migrate, it crawls confidently to the opening, expecting to swim back out the way it came in. That's when it discovers the ghastly price of that time of perfect security: it's grown too big to fit through the neck of the bottle! In a terrible ironic twist, that safe shelter now becomes a death chamber; its protective shield will be its coffin.

Albert Holtz OSB

26

The surfer is my favourite example of the disciplined wild man, the man who has a perfectly balanced ascetical-mystical life. Check out his style. He gets up early in the morning. That's a tough ascetical act of self-denial. Then he attends carefully and reverently to his board, polishing and waxing it with love. Next he puts the board, this burden of love, this sacred tool, on his head and walks silently and solitary to the sea. There he faces a lonely and forbidding beach hardly perceptible in the fog. He then plunges into cold water, works his way out into the deeps against the waves, and now comes the keenest ascetical act of all: he waits; no impulsive action, no rush, no rash moves. He looks, listens, sees the distant waters, watching intently, contemplatively for the right wave, letting all the others go by. Finally, he sees the big wave coming. Deftly and adroitly he moves into position – timing is so important – not to master the wave, but to meet it and become one. They meet. He ... surrenders himself ... and he rides ... in utter delight and sheer ecstasy. That is the mystical goal of a surfer's asceticism.

Such exquisite delight in God's cascading glory.

William McNamara OCD

27

Life in common always has its asceticism. Contemplative union with God both requires and causes self-denial. That very idea raises defenses in our culture; we do not want to hear the word. Monastic living witnesses not only to its necessity, but even more to its potential. Self-denial is better spelled self-transcendence, since its purpose is the going beyond that opens out to new and deeper life. What dies is exaggerated individualism; what flourishes, a love that strengthens one's ego and a love for others that enriches all in the family of God.

Marie Beha OSC

28

When we draw water from a well, it can happen that we inadvertently also bring up a frog. When we acquire virtues we can

sometimes find ourselves involved with the vices which are im-
perceptibly interwoven with them. What I mean is this. Gluttony
can be caught up with hospitality; lust with love; cunning with
discernment; malice with prudence; duplicity, procrastination,
slovenliness, stubbornness, wilfulness and disobedience with
meekness; refusal to learn with silence; conceit with joy; laziness
with hope; hasty condemnation with love again; despondency
and indolence with tranquillity; sarcasm with chastity; familiarity with lowliness. And behind all the virtues follows vainglory
as a salve, or rather a poison, for everything.

John Climacus

29

There follows: 'You are my friends.' How great is the mercy of
our Creator! We are unworthy servants, and yet we are called
friends. How great an honor it is for human beings to be the
friends of God. But having heard of the proud distinction, learn
also of the hardship of the struggle for it: 'If you do what I command you'. It is as though he said: You are delighted about the
final outcome. Weigh well the efforts by which it is reached. '...
I have called you friends, for all that I have heard from my Father
I have made known to you.' When we love these heavenly things
of which we hear, we already know what we love, for the love
itself is the knowledge.

Gregory the Great

30

A Sufi tells of the old, old woman who was on pilgrimage to
the shrine at the top of the mountain at the height of the mon-
soon season. 'You will never be able to climb that mountain in
weather like this', the innkeeper said on a dark, wet night. 'Oh,

my friend', the old woman said, 'that will be no problem at all. My heart has been there all my life. Now it is simply a matter of taking my body there as well.' It is time now in religious history to form for pilgrimage; to ignore the storms around us and to press on, press on, press on to where our hearts await our bodies this very day.

Joan Chittister OSB

31

I pray, O God, that I may know you and love you, so that I may rejoice in you. And if I cannot do so fully in this life may I progress gradually until it comes to fullness. Let the knowledge of you grow in me here, and there [in heaven] be made complete; let your love grow in me here and there be made complete, so that here my joy may be great in hope, and there be complete in reality.

Anselm of Canterbury

February

Seeking guidance

Beginners who intend to make any progress worth mentioning ... should reveal the secrets of their hearts to those whose office it is to exercise a compassionate and sympathetic care for the weak.

Basil, Long Rules 26

I

We are a generation that yearns for wisdom figures, heroes and heroines, ammas and abbas [as in Desert Mothers and Fathers] who will show us the way. While maintaining fierce independence, we desire interdependence and community. We want our lives to have depth of meaning and purpose. We want to be connected. We secretly want someone to challenge us toward the transcendent.

Laura Swan OSB

2

The majority of these seekers [young people going to India in the 1960s and 70s] forget to begin by emptying their souls of all that is useless and extraneous, and by opening themselves to their true depths where alone it is possible to receive India's message. This message gushes forth on all sides in India; from the temples and holy places and, above all, from the holy men, who are by no means scarce, whatever may be said to the contrary; but one must know how to hear the message and how to meet these true spiritual masters. In truth there is passivity and passivity. There is one form of passivity which is all acceptance and receptivity, all 'listening', like a radio set perfectly tuned and free from interference, ready to pick up the waves transmitted through space. There is another form of passivity, which is unfortunately the more common one, which refuses every attempt at assimilation and has not the least desire to clear the mind of prejudices and preoccupations: if one does not even bother to open the shutters how can one expect even the midday sun to come into the room?

Abhishiktananda (Henri le Saux OSB*)*

3

'Acquire inward peace,' said St Seraphim, 'and a multitude of people around you will find their salvation.' Such is the role of spiritual fatherhood. Establish yourself in God; then you can bring others to God's presence. A man must learn to be alone, he must listen in the stillness of his own heart to the wordless speech of the Spirit, and so discover the truth about himself and God. Then his work to others will be a word of power, because it is a word out of silence.

What Nikos Kazantzakis said of the almond tree is true also of the starets [spiritual guide]: 'I said to the almond tree, "Sister, speak to me of God", and the almond tree blossomed.'

Kallistos Ware

4

Augustine notes that appropriate reproof is one of the benefits that we can expect from genuine friendship. If I were engaging in behavior that is liable to be damaging, I would hope that a friend would help me to see the error of my ways. I make mistakes, some of which are unimportant. A few, however, may have results that I would gladly prevent. If somebody else is able to open my eyes to what is going wrong and to encourage me to take contrary action, then I am greatly blessed. If I have ongoing access to such a resource, then I can be reasonably relaxed about the choices I make, knowing that if delusion ever gets the better of me, a friend will spot the danger and alert me to it. Correction or putting right is a benefit rather than an added burden.

Michael Casey OCSO

5

Abba Macarius was asked, 'How should one pray?' The old man said, 'There is no need to make long discourses; it is enough to stretch out one's hands and say, "Lord, as you will, and as you know, have mercy." And if the conflict grows fiercer say, "Lord, help!" He knows very well what we need and he shews us his mercy.'

Macarius the Great

6

In the early days of my life on Mt Athos I remember asking one of the hermits to talk to me about prayer. Discerning in my request a wish to hear about prayer at its most sublime, he replied, 'Let us discuss what we are capable of. To talk of what is beyond us would be idle chatter.' I felt ashamed but still ventured to say, 'I really do want to know about more perfect prayer – prayer that surpasses me. Not because I am pretentious. No. But because it seems to me vital to glimpse a guiding star to check whether I am on the right path. In ancient times mariners took their bearings by an incredibly remote star. In the same way I should like to have a true criterion, however out of reach, so that I shall not be content with the little I have so far discovered.' The holy man agreed that this was not only permissible but right and proper.

Archimandrite Sophrony (Sakharov)

7

It is basic to leadership that we can only take others over ground we have ourselves covered.

In order to do this, each of us has a need, almost an imperative, to confront the unknown which lies coiled in the centre of our heart's labyrinth, and it is the role of the spiritual guide to help us to do this. We have an urge to drink from a hidden spring in the secret place within ourselves where both our treasure and our rubbish are stored. Our instinct tells us that, psychologically and spiritually, this is the route to liberation.

Frances Teresa OSC

8

We crave for spiritual security, or rather the feeling of security; real security is what God wants us to have and that can only be when we have let go our own securities, which are illusory, and rely on him alone.

The craving for spiritual guidance may well form one of these illusory securities. We want to be assured that what is happening in our prayer is all right, we want to be given definite guidelines so that we can feel safe. 'Direction' ... can be dangerous. For one thing it presumes not only an intimate knowledge of the one concerned but also a knowledge of God and his mysterious ways on the part of the director. Friendly advice on the basis of equality is one thing, to put one's soul in the hands of someone else is another. Many people have come into the catholic church or have gladly stayed in her because she represented security in this insecure world, with her incontrovertible authority. Now that this authority is being questioned they are upset and resentful. They have to ask themselves if they are not more concerned with feeling safe than with loving God.

Ruth Burrows

9

Taking direction from another opens us to the wisdom of the world around us. It frees us to go on learning in life. To think that it is our responsibility to have all the answers is a terrible burden. It is an even worse burden to believe that we have those answers.

People often labour under the illusion that not knowing something is a sign of failure. In so doing, they suppress the gifts of those in their care by their unhappy dash to prove their competence and authority. They set themselves up to fail as well. Those who believe they have nothing left to learn from anybody and dare anyone to try and teach them are describing the size of their own souls – small. Everybody has something to learn from somebody – and learning is never easy.

Joan Chittister OSB

10

A brother asked Abba Poemen, 'If a brother has a little money which belongs to me, do you advise me to ask him for it?' The old man said to him, 'Ask him for it once.' The brother said to him, 'And then what should I do? For I cannot control my thoughts.' The old man said to him, 'Be quiet and do not think about it. But do not distress your brother.'

Abba Poemen

11

At times we so rigidly define our lives that we cease to be open to new perspectives. Anything that feeds into our current concerns is accepted as relevant; everything else is dismissed as of lesser importance. So many significant issues are put 'on hold' because we do not feel it is necessary that we deal with them right away. As a result, we do not build the infrastructure on which 'relevant' insights will depend. Perhaps we hear the word and understand it intellectually. Because we do not carry it around, bridges are not built between the text and daily life. Not everything is immediately relevant. Sometimes we have to juggle two apparently divergent themes in our minds until some sort of connectedness links them. Suddenly the next step becomes evident. It takes time and it demands of us the capacity to let God's word untidy our lives in the short term. If we can live with this divine chaos, it will eventually produce consistency and harmony not based on denial and repression, but coming from the courageous effort to eliminate whatever is incompatible with the following of Christ.

Michael Casey OCSO

12

A brother asked a hermit, 'Tell me something good that I may do it and live by it.' The hermit said, 'God alone knows what is good. But I have heard that one of the hermits asked the great Nesteros, who was a friend of Antony, "What good work shall I do?" and he replied, "Surely all works please God equally? Scripture says, Abraham was hospitable and God was with him; Elijah loved quiet and God was with him; David was humble and God was with him." So whatever you find you are drawn to in following God's will, do it and let your heart be at peace.'

A Desert Father

13

There is a story about a Chinese village once threatened by drought. Unless the rains came quickly the villagers were going to starve. In vain, they tried everything. Finally, in desperation, they sent a great distance for a famous Rainmaker. He came. Immediately he asked for a straw hut to be built for him outside the village and for rations of food and water. He also asked to be left alone. He then disappeared into the hut. On the 4th day it rained, just in time to save the village. But one man said to him, 'How did you do it? What ceremony do you perform?' He replied, 'When I came to your village, I was so out of sorts that I had first to put things right inside myself. I never really got round to the ceremony of rainmaking.'

James McCaffrey OCD

14

[Amma Theodora] said that a teacher ought to be a stranger to the desire for domination, vain-glory, and pride; one should not be able to fool him by flattery, nor blind him by gifts, nor conquer him by the stomach, nor dominate him by anger; but he should be patient, gentle and humble as far as possible; he must be tested and without partisanship, full of concern, and a lover of souls.

Amma Theodora

15

God's voice is not always heard in thunder, nor is it obtrusive like advertising, but it is often very soft and unobtrusive and needs to be listened to with love and in recollection.

The Rule of Benedict begins with a dialogue between the newcomer and the human mediator of the Word of God. This reminds us of the process so often described in the [*Sayings of the Desert Fathers*]. The question of the young person is answered by the elder or father with a word, an admonition; and this word comes from Sacred Scripture or from his own experience with Scripture.

Aquinata Böckmann OSB

16

He is entirely alone who is without a friend.

But what happiness, what security, what joy to have someone to whom you dare to speak on terms of equality as to another self; one to whom you need to have no fear to confess your failings; one to whom you can unblushingly make known progress you have made in the spiritual life; one to whom you can entrust all the secrets of your heart and before whom you can place all your plans! What, therefore, is more pleasant than so to unite to oneself the spirit of another and of two to form one, that no boasting is thereafter to be feared, no suspicion to be dreaded, no correction of one by the other to cause pain, no praise on the part of one to bring a charge of adulation from the other.

Aelred of Rievaulx

17

It is true that superiors cannot be all things to all people ... Real engagement with someone else's struggles is not always possible and does not always work. But if the very essence of the office is a relationship of love, that relationship runs far deeper and should be evident in much more than juridical and administrative tasks.

... Benedict's comprehensive understanding of Christian leadership defies reduction to a list of tasks. He ends up emphasizing the qualities of the office-holder rather than the duties of the office. Spiritual leadership depends on spiritual authority, which finally is not about office or title but about the recognizable presence of the Holy Spirit in one's life.

Columba Stewart OSB

18

A brother at Scetis committed a fault. A council was called to which Abba Moses was invited, but he refused to go to it. Then the priest sent someone to say to him, 'Come, for everyone is waiting for you.' So he got up and went. He took a leaking jug, filled it with water and carried it with him. The others came out to meet him and said to him, 'What is this, Father?' The old man said to them, 'My sins run out behind me, and I do not see them, and today I am coming to judge the errors of another.' When they heard that they said no more to the brother but forgave him.

A Desert Father

19

Tradition is not what *has been* done but what is *being* lived in continuity with the past and in a hopeful thrust towards the future. The word itself, *traditio*, means a 'passing on', a 'transmission'. Christian faith is effectively lost, though the structures of Christianity may remain powerful for a while, when tradition becomes archaic rather than a contemporary reappropriation and projection forward. What is being regained and passed on is not something that can replace the necessity of our personally experiencing it. The life of a tradition is precisely this multiple personal experience forming and awakening the ecclesial reality.

John Main OSB

20

The uneducated and foolish regard instruction as ridiculous and do not want to receive it, because it would show up their uncouthness, and they want everyone to be like themselves. Likewise those

who are dissipated in their life and habits are anxious to prove
that everyone else is worse than themselves, seeking to present
themselves as innocent in comparison with all the sinners around
them ...

Those who aim to practise the life of virtue and holiness should
not incur condemnation by pretending to a piety which they do
not possess. But like painters and sculptors they should manifest
their virtue and holiness through their works.

Antony the Great (attributed)

21

There is another attitude towards a person, which consists in saying: 'I know very little about you. I know that there is in you a
chaos of things that has not yet acquired either an orientation or
a form; but I have faith in the dynamic possibilities of this chaos,
because God is at work in the midst of it.' Then I recognize you
for what you are. I accept you, not as you are, but as you are plus
all the inner chaos. I make an act of faith, and I help you to emerge
from your own chaos as you are to be, without my knowing what
you will become. That is the attitude of a true spiritual guide. He
doesn't try to make beings in his own image, but tries, almost by
incantation, to make rise from the chaos all that is divine, all that
is human, all that is capable of entering into the harmony of the
kingdom of God. That is the way God treats chaos. He creates us
with a world of things unresolved and he calls us.

Anthony Bloom

22

The Sufi masters recount this tale:
    'May I become your disciple?' the seeker asked.
    'You are only a disciple because your eyes are closed. The day

you open them, you will see that there is nothing you can learn from me,' the holy one answered.

'Then what is a master for?' the seeker asked.

'The purpose of a master,' the holy one said, 'is to bring you to the point where you know the uselessness of having one.'

Joan Chittister OSB

23

The fact that I am a monk and you are a layman is of no importance. The Lord listens equally to the monk and to the man of the world provided both are true believers. He looks for a heart full of true faith into which to send his Spirit. For the heart of a man is capable of containing the Kingdom of God. The Holy Spirit and the Kingdom of God are one.

I have now told you everything. Go in peace. May the Lord and his Holy Mother be with you always. Amen.

Seraphim of Sarov

24

Abba Poemen said that Abba Ammonas said, 'A man can spend his whole time carrying an axe without succeeding in cutting down the tree; while another, with experience of tree-felling, brings down the tree with a few blows.' He said the axe is discernment.

Abba Ammonas

25

The chain-link fence got there first. By the time the sumac tree started growing beside it, the fence was simply a given, like the ocean or the Alps. The fence made it impossible for the sapling to grow into a normal sumac with branches arranged neatly along a perfectly straight trunk.

The tree started to grow as best it could, though, accepting the soccer field as a fact of life. It poled its branches through the diamond-shaped holes and wrapped itself around the heavy wires until they became part of its very self. In the process its trunk, as thick as my wrist, got twisted and gnarled ...

As I look at all its peculiar twists and knots, it occurs to me that this tree is a living lesson about a deep spiritual reality: true happiness doesn't come from being perfect.

Albert Holtz OSB

26

We don't have all the answers. We do, thank God, have some answers ... But there are questions, lots of questions. And it is good to live in the question. A pat answer is closed, it is finished; that's it. It goes nowhere and leaves little room for hope. A question, the mystery, opens the space for us. It is full of possibility. It gives hope of life and ever more abundant life. Our faith, solid as it might be, is full of questions. And therefore full of life and hope.

Basil Pennington OCSO

27

Many times while I was at prayer, I would keep asking for what seemed good to me. I kept insisting on my own request, unreasonably putting pressure on the will of God. I simply would not leave it up to his Providence to arrange what he knew would turn out for my profit. Finally, when I obtained my request I became greatly chagrined at having been so stubborn about getting my own way, for in the end the matter did not turn out to be what I had fancied it would.

What else is there that is good besides God alone? Therefore let us cast all our concerns upon him and it will be well with us. Certainly, he who is wholly good is necessarily the kind of person who gives only good gifts.

Evagrius Ponticus

28

Abba Pambo asked Abba Anthony, 'What ought I to do?' and the old man said to him, 'Do not trust your own righteousness, do not worry about the past, but control your tongue and your stomach.'

Abba Anthony

29

Humility, the Rule of Benedict teaches, requires first and fore-most what the ancients called the *memoria dei*, 'the awareness of God,' at all times, in all places, at the center of all things. It is so easy in a patriarchal society to make ourselves gods of the tiny little kingdoms we occupy. We climb very small ladders and then assume that we have risen to the heights of our humanity. The realization that God is god and that we are not requires seri-ous reflection. Striving for all the tops of all the pyramids in the world will not change the fact that no person ever really reaches the top of anything and that the real acme of creation lies deep within the soul and waits for us to bow before it in awareness and in praise. Those whose lives are lived without listening to their hearts, those who make themselves, their work, their status, their money their god, never find the God of the universe, who waits quietly within for us to exhaust our compulsive race to nowhere.

Unlike everything else in a patriarchal world, God, according to the Rule of Benedict, is not a goal to be reached; God is a presence to be recognized.

Joan Chittister OSB

March

Living with others

Community life offers more blessings than can be fully
or easily enumerated.

Basil, Long Rules 7

I

A brother was restless in his community and he was often irritated. So he said, 'I will go and live somewhere by myself. I will not be able to talk or listen to anyone and so I shall be at peace, and my passionate anger will cease.' He went out and lived alone in a cave. But one day he filled his jug with water and put it on the ground. Suddenly it happened to fall over. He filled it again, and again it fell. This happened a third time. In a rage he snatched up the jug and smashed it. Coming to his senses, he knew that the demon of anger had mocked him, and he said, 'Here am I by myself, and he has beaten me. I will return to the community. Wherever you live, you need effort and patience and above all God's help.' So he got up, and went back.

A Desert Father

2

The Twelve Steps
of Humility

* Recognize the presence of God
* Accept the will of God
* Accept spiritual direction
* Persevere
* Acknowledge faults
* Live simply
* Be honest about yourself
* Be willing to learn from others
* Listen to people
* Speak kindly to others

* Accept others the way they are
* Be centered and serene

Joan Chittister OSB

3

A brother asked an old man: What is humility? And the old man said: To do good to those who hurt you. The brother said: If you cannot go that far, what should you do? The old man replied: Get away from them and keep your mouth shut.

A Desert Father

4

The hard work of obedience happens in the dailiness of our relationships.

It is reflected in the details of returning the car keys on time, signing out and leaving a phone number. In accepting assigned 'obediences', bells, dishes, cleaning, in turning in budgets and balancing checkbooks as requested. Only with faith is there spiritual significance in having to ask permission, but in itself it reminds us of the commitment we made. We have thrown our lot in with others. We can become quite mystical in talking about obedience, but it is the little things that provide the real test of our authenticity as monastics living under a rule and a prioress in our search for God.

Christine Vladimiroff OSB

5

There are some individuals who have a natural bent toward anger, yet who are accustomed so to restrain and overcome this passion that they never give way to vices which scripture testifies dissolve and break friendship. However, they may occasionally offend a friend by a thoughtless word or act or by a zeal that fails in discretion. If it happens that we have received such men into our friendship, we must bear with them patiently. And since their affection toward us is established with certainty, if then there is any excess in word or action, this ought to be put up with as being in a friend, or at least our admonition of his fault ought to be administered painlessly and even pleasantly.

Aelred of Rievaulx

6

After a sort of honeymoon within the community the faults and limitations of the brethren begin to appear, and to contrast strongly with the ideal community we have envisaged. They will appear as obstacles on the spiritual path until we accept the truth about ourselves. If we are to form a real bond with others, we must know ourselves and our limitations and faults. We are no better than others. We too need mercy and if the truth be known we need it more than others. We must learn to know the tender mercy of God which pursues us even when we sin. God's love is forgiveness. And we too are called on to show each other the same forgiving love.

André Louf OCSO

7

Everyone in the community should take turns in serving at
the table. (RB 35)

A shared service at table is Benedict's way of pointing towards a
fundamental equality in the community.

What does this fundamental equality actually mean? We need
to be careful here, because it might be read as a levelling down,
of ensuring that those at the top don't 'get too big for their boots'
by making everybody do something that nobody wants to do at
all. It is in fact a way of emphasizing the distinction that must
exist in a Benedictine community between vocation and function. It must be the case that the functions of different monks
vary according to the needs of a particular monastery at a particular time and also because of the natural diversity of gifts and
skills. To imagine a community where everybody did the same
work, undifferentiated by ability, would be to create a monster of
quite un-Christian dimensions. But we cannot stop at diversity,
for monks are bound together by a common vocation in which
everybody shares.

Timothy Wright OSB

8

One of the most characteristic American ways of evading the
identity problem is *conformism*, running with the herd, the refusal of solitude, flight from loneliness. This exists even in monasteries and can create a serious problem if, for renunciation and
inner solitude, it tries to substitute a false atmosphere of collec-
tive euphoria and corrupt our cenobitic life with a vapid 'togetherness'. Togetherness is not 'community'. To love our brother we
must first respect him in his own authentic personal reality, and
we cannot do this if we have not attained a basic self-respect and
mature identity ourselves.

Are our efforts to be more 'communal' and to be more of a 'family' really genuine or are they only new ways to be intolerant of the solitude and integrity of the individual person? Are we simply trying to submerge and absorb him, and keep him from finding an identity that might express itself in dissent and in a desire for greater solitude? Are we simply trying to guard against his entering a 'desert' of questioning and paradox that will disturb our own complacencies?

Louis [Thomas] Merton

9

Some old men came to see Abba Poemen, and said to him: Tell us, when we see brothers dozing during the sacred office, should we pinch them so they will stay awake? The old man said to them: Actually, if I saw a brother sleeping, I would put his head on my knees and let him rest.

Abba Poemen

10

In every human being there is a tension between the lure of the safe and certain on the one hand, and the challenge of the unknown and risky on the other. Our lives are shaped by the ebb and flow of the struggle between these two forces inside us ... I call them 'mastery' and 'intimacy.' ...

Mastery is the approach to life in which I impose my will on situations and people, using my power to make things happen just the way I want. Intimacy, on the other hand, means the willingness to deal with what is given, without having to change every situation to suit me or to fix what's 'wrong' with every person I meet.

Albert Holtz OSB

11

There is a fasting from injurious acts, and there is a fasting from injurious thoughts, if we use the word in the sense the desert fathers gave it, i.e. the thought plus its emotional charge.

This fasting from thoughts may take the form of an interior vigilance over what thoughts we allow into our mind, rejecting thoughts of judgement, criticism, violence, and accepting those of understanding, patience, love. It is in our power, usually, to fix our attention on the good qualities of a person or a situation, and not on the less good. Our thoughts will then be thoughts of peace and our acts will follow. We can choose to counteract any movements of aggressivity towards others, by deliberately, in our minds, affirming the other who annoys us in what he is and can become in Christ. All this within our own heart. The acts will follow. This is a form of intimate self-denial, a fast that pleases God who is love. For all non-love flows from love of self.

A Carthusian

12

Under all the pomp and steel, despite all the money and guns, beyond all the status and roles, the world, we all know down deep, is a very vulnerable place. Nothing stands completely safe from the exigencies of living, the dailiness of survival, the fragility of life even at its most benign. Whatever our securities, the sense of nakedness, of alert, of potential danger never leaves us. We are vulnerable from all sides, in and out, up and down, past, present, and future. We fear vulnerability. It takes a great deal of living to discover that, actually, vulnerability comes to us more as friend than as enemy. Vulnerability may be the greatest strength we have.

Vulnerability bonds us to one another, and makes us a community in league with life. Because we need one another, we live looking for good in others, without which we ourselves can not survive, will not grow, can not become what we ourselves have the potential to be. Vulnerability is the gift given to us to enable us to embed ourselves in the universe.

Joan Chittister OSB

13

Lots of people operate reasonably well when they are 'in the world' with their own space and a range of safety valves. When they embrace a common life they may find that many of the avenues of recuperation that they hitherto took for granted are unavailable. Pressure builds up, and some of the residue of past history begins to create a ferment inside them. This they attribute to the malign ambience or the actions of those around them. Before long, instead of reading what is happening inside themselves, they begin to project onto their neighbors the disturbance they feel. Blame takes over: Difference is seen as insensitivity, and everyday thoughtlessness is interpreted as deliberate malice. The ideal of community, so long desired, evaporates before the reality. Mutuality may be an admirable goal but it seems that it cannot be realized in this place, and certainly not with these people.

Michael Casey OCSO

14

One day when Abba John was going up to Scetis with some other brothers, their guide lost his way for it was night-time. So the brothers said to Abba John, 'What shall we do, abba, in order not to die wandering about, for the brother has lost the way?' The old man said to them, 'If we speak to him, he will be filled with grief and shame. But look here, I will pretend to be ill and say I cannot walk any more; then we can stay here till the dawn.' This he did. The others said, 'We will not go on either, but we will stay with you.' They sat there until the dawn, and in this way they did not upset the brother.

Abba John

15

In guilt the other is experienced not as a presence but as pressure. Under this pressure I feel a powerlessness to love. The felt powerlessness to love is the very nerve of guilt. Because my root inclination is to enter into relationships, I tend to interpret the unlovableness of someone as something I am producing by strangling this inclination. This makes me feel guilty. Although there is only a limited sense in which it is true to say that the unlovableness of another is my fault, it is something I can never be happy about. This unhappiness is a feeling of guilt.

When something is going badly wrong with an intimate relationship, we experience this 'ugliness of the other' in an intense way. Suddenly the beloved can appear hateful. This is due to the sudden failure of my normal love-current, which leaves the beloved before me in all his or her closeness and involvement in my life, while I am powerless to respond. Guilt is acute when the intimate other becomes alien. In all guilt, the other appears alien. Guilt is when the other changes from partner to alien. Because partnership is natural and congenial to me, is the way my life wants to flow, this 'alienation' of the partner is experienced by me as a contradiction with myself. This self-contradiction, this inner friction of the spirit, is the experience of guilt.

Sebastian Moore OSB

16

For many women, naming and confronting the injustice perpetuated against them is more difficult than enduring it. Often confronting injustice results in a shift in relationship. The unknown can be quite fearful until the self is explored and familiar. Familiar pain can feel more comfortable than the risk of an unknown healing process. When we know our strengths, we can converse with our fears. Conflicts and difficult situations deepen our awareness of personal triggers; those areas where our reactions are out of proportion to the situation. Seeking resolution and reconciliation matures us and strengthens our interior discipline.

Laura Swan OSB

17

Perhaps the community thinking of the Irish monks is nowhere more clearly revealed than on the sculptured high crosses. Christ is never alone on them and the sculptors seem to have been obsessed with the text 'Where two or three are gathered together in my name ...' Many of the scenes depicted are related to community: Paul and Anthony having a meal, the three children in the fiery furnace, the twelve apostles, Noah's ark, and the multiplication of the loaves and fishes. Many of the crosses were capped with a miniature oratory. The crosses themselves were a community effort, even if a single sculptor carved some of them. The Book of Kells seems to have been the work of a team of monks, and at least two artists were responsible for its finest page, the Chi-Rho carpet page.

Ciaran O'Sabhaois OCSO

18

An ascetic brother who did not eat bread went to visit a great old man. Now some other visitors were there, and for their sake the old man had done a little cooking. They sat down to eat, and the ascetic put only a few soaked peas in front of him and ate them.

When they arose from table, the old man took him aside and said to him, 'Brother, when you go to visit someone, do not let your way of life be seen. But if you want to hold to your *ascesis*, remain in your cell and never come out of it.' Taught by this saying of the old man's, he learnt to do as everyone else when he was with the brethren.

A Desert Father

19

Benedict's insight into the psychology of murmuring ['this resistant or whiny attitude'] helps us to understand what is often described as 'passive-aggressive' behaviour. We know someone who always smiles, conforms to the rules, perhaps even poses as an exemplary monk or nun, while dumbfounding others with occasional flashes of the anger concealed behind the obedient facade. The anger flares out in small but concentrated doses which are often not immediately recognized for the poison they are. The disappointments and resentments that create such poison build up over a lifetime and become harder and harder to salve. By insisting so strongly on the ban against murmuring, Benedict wants his followers to deal with the memories and emotions which make them prone to vicious talk. He also helps to name the resistances we all experience, the calculations and hesitations that accompany every response to a question or assignment.

Columba Stewart OSB

20

Nor does the fact that there were many hermits in Ireland take from the appreciation of community living. ... Even as hermits the Irish often started a new community. St Ciarán of Seir had a wild boar and a fox as companions. Br Fox got sick of the vegetable diet and ate the saint's sandals. St Colman had a cock to wake him for vigils and a fly to mark the lines on the psalter when he stopped for a 'sacred silence'. When he complained to St Colm on the death of his friends he was reproached for his worldliness. But the cat seemed to be the favourite of these men. There is the famous poem on Pangur Ban, and cats appear on the Cross of Muireadach at Monasterboic and in the Book of Kells.

Ciaran O'Sabhaois OCSO

21

It is surprising how much togetherness one needs to save aloneness from deteriorating into loneliness. Here lies the root of monastic community. Solitude and togetherness make one another possible. Take away solitude and togetherness becomes subhuman gregariousness; take away togetherness and solitude becomes desolation. Community can only exist in the tension between solitude and togetherness. The delicate balance between solitude and togetherness will determine what kind of community it shall be. In the togetherness community of which married life is the prototype, togetherness is the measure of solitude: each partner must have as much solitude as he or she needs for rich and full togetherness. In the solitude community of monastic life, solitude is the measure of togetherness: here each partner must have just enough togetherness to enrich and support his solitude. Monks in community help one another in love to cultivate and sustain genuine aloneness.

David Steindl-Rast OSB

22

If chairmen of committees and those in seats of authority were forced to write out personally in longhand everything they wanted to communicate to others, no doubt they would choose their words with greater care.

Kallistos Ware

23

I have presented Saint Benedict as a relatively optimistic personality who is inclined to trust people. It seems to me that a school that claims to carry on the values of Benedict must retain something of this attitude. There is plenty of pessimism at work in our society today; if there were not, we in the United States would not be the only major western nation to employ the death penalty, nor would we lead the western world in percentage of citizens in prison. I realize that these are hard questions, and no easy answers are available. Even within Christianity, some traditions are more or less optimistic than others. ...

I think it is accurate to say that, when it comes to people, Benedict is optimistic. Which reminds me of a line from an extraordinary movie entitled *Harold and Maude* that tells of a romance between an 18-year-old boy and an 82-year-old woman. The latter is the star of the show, a really nice person. At one point Harold says in amazement: 'You really like people, don't you?' 'Why not?' says Maude, 'after all, they are my species!'

Terence Kardong OSB

24

Without solitude there can be no real people. The more you discover what a person is, and experience what a human relationship requires in order to remain profound, fruitful, and a source of growth and development, the more you discover that you are alone – and that the measure of your solitude is the measure of your capacity for communion. The measure of your awareness of God's transcendent call to each person is the measure of your capacity for intimacy with others. If you do not realize that the persons to whom you are relating are each called to an eternal transcendent relationship that transcends everything else, how can you relate intimately to another at his center from your center?

John Eudes Bamberger OCSO

25

It would be fair to say that Benedictines are still in a transitional period of learning how obedience and humility can be central monastic values applied maturely and honestly. Reactions against narrow models of obedience and destructive understandings of humility can go and have gone too far in the direction of prizing autonomy above all else. Obedience has typically become a process of discernment, a real gain in terms of mature ownership of a decision but also potentially a means of stalling or resisting an unwelcome invitation. Humility is a difficult concept for those who have suffered from misapplications of it in the past, yet the kind of keen self-awareness that Benedict encourages has never been more necessary than it is now in modern cultures full of fantasies about who and what we ought to be.

Columba Stewart OSB

26

When television first began to be widely commercial in the 1950s the leading American theorist on communications flatly predicted that it would never be a success because 'people would have to sit in a dark room and ignore each other'. One might wonder how far that attitude has affected our religious sense of community?
... In the long run the challenge will be to discover a sense

of community living that binds together the older familial style of community with the newer style of spontaneous and heightened psychological interchange. Both possess strong values: the former, a powerful sense of physical togetherness in work and prayer, a set of common goals built up through repeated sharing, and the virtue of perseverance; the latter, an emphasis on the value of emotional support and a true recreational element in community. The merging of these two styles will affect all types of societal living today: the family, the social organization, the local parish, as well as the monastery.

Matthias Neuman OSB

27

Energy, new life, relationships extend far beyond their point of origin. It is now believed that space is filled with so-called 'fields' of connections. We have long been familiar with the all-pervasive fields of gravity and magnetism. ... In human relationships also, there are comparable fields of energy. One can actually feel different kinds of fields when walking into a home or church or community. Because of attitudes and behaviors of individuals in the community, a person can almost tangibly touch an invisible field of energy: hospitality, openness, peace, friendliness, or tension, suspicion, coldness, rigidity.

Ruth Fox OSB

28

Friendship presupposes both equality and complementarity. It feeds on this diversity which enables each of the friends to give something to the other. Likewise in the common life this exchange of different charisms can nourish mutual love. There are, however, many differences between people – the character of each, his experience before he came to the monastery. The monks come from different backgrounds. Perhaps one was a student, another a worker, another in the army. One may be from the city, another from the countryside. At the time of St Benedict there were free men and slaves. What matters is that the monastery be truly ecumenical; it does not obliterate differences but leads them to convergence in Christ. In this connection St Benedict reminds us that we all serve the same master and the one Lord (RB 61:10). In fact these differences provide grounds for sharing and for mutual respect, which cannot but be for the strengthening of the community.

André Louf OCSO

29

The capacity to open ourselves to others, to know and love them, is something we receive first of all from them as a gratuitous gift. For a child, this is obvious: the smile of its mother awakens the child's smile. But we have never finished being born throughout our life; there is always a child in us which has access to its full human reality only by means of the warmth of a human welcome and love. When this is lacking, when we become isolated, without deep contact with a human being, sooner or later something freezes in the inmost part of our heart, we die little by little from not loving.

A Carthusian

30

The third form of countercultural spiritual combat is community life ... Our Rule spells out this communitarian vision in terms of a sharing of goods and life, an egalitarian style of life, communal-dialogical discernment, and a respect for the individual.

This communitarian life, signalled in our Carmelite Rule, is itself a countercultural protest against the commodity form with its objectifying of the person through dominative and dehumanizing relationships, its lack of care and respect, its enslavement of freedom, and its idolizing of competition, achievement, and control. In turn, such a communitarian life witnesses to the values of the personal form: the intrinsic worth of persons, freedom, detachment, generosity, justice, peace, forgiveness, healing, compassion, and the empowering of those who are least.

Donald W. Buggert, o carm

31

Others are the bridge to our own development. They make up what is wanting in us. They demand new insights in us, new awareness, new skills of patience and acceptance. They require us to overcome our revulsions, to risk a wild trust, to take down the barriers in our lives. They teach us to let differences in so that we do not all die of the breathless white space with which we surround ourselves. They enable us to take on the heart of God for them.

Most of all, other people teach us that no one has the right to take up all the space in life. There are other ideas, other ways of doing things, other needs and desires than ours in life. It is a painful moment, this time of testing the truth of what we say we believe. It comes at odd times: when we are tempted to ignore the appeals for alms because we are tired of giving to the 'shiftless.' It comes when we are intent on having our own way. It comes when we resist the chance to hire women and minorities. It comes when we are tempted to tell the latest ethnic joke that ridicules and reduces to dust a whole class of people.

Joan Chittister osb

April

Going to work

Then they are truly monastics when they live by the labour of their
hands, like our forebears and the apostles.

Rule of Benedict, Chapter 48

I

For Benedict, work is an essential element of monastic life. 'They are truly monks if they live by the labor of their hands' (Benedictine Rule 48.8). Work, whether it be manual, intellectual or in some cases pastoral, is the context in which the creative capacity or the ability to collaborate with others and with God becomes evident. A monk must learn to work seriously in the service of the community, or, in the name of the community, in the service of the Church and society.

Work does not fill this role of forming a person if it is amateurish in character or if it becomes, as can easily happen, an occasion for seeking power and the expression of self will.

Armand Veilleux OCSO

2

An old man said, 'If someone lives in a place and does not reap the fruit which that place affords, it will drive him away because he has not known how to work there.'

A Desert Father

3

In the Prologue of his Rule for Monks (verses 14–20), St Benedict imagines God turning up in a crowded marketplace. He describes God looking for workmen to take on, but he does not say what the job is or what he requires. He just asks who wants a life, or to see good days – some recruiting pitch! But God does not actually have any particular job in mind; it is not a question of getting any specific task done. He just asks who wants a life. It is just a question of living well.

The real task, then, is life.

David Foster OSB

4

Amma Syncletica said: If you happen to live in a community, do not move to another place, for it will harm you greatly. If a bird leaves her eggs, they never hatch. So also the monk and the nun grow cold and dead in faith by going from place to place.

Amma Syncletica

5

The spiritual life is not a specialized part of daily life. Everything you do in the day, from washing to eating breakfast, having meetings, driving to work, solving problems, making more problems for yourself once you have solved them, watching television or deciding instead to read, going to a restaurant or a movie or going to church, *everything* you do is your spiritual life. It is only a matter of how consciously you do these ordinary things, how attentive you are to the opportunities they offer for growth, for enjoyment, and how mindfully, how selflessly, how compassionately you perform them.

Laurence Freeman OSB

6

Work makes time worthwhile. Time is all we have to make our
lives bright-colored, warm, and rich. Time spent on an artificial
high is time doomed to failure. Time spent amassing what I cannot possibly use is time wasted. Time spent in gray, dry aimless-
ness is a prison of the thickest walls. But good work that leaves
the world softer and fuller and better than even before is the stuff
of which human satisfaction and spiritual value are made. There
will come a moment in life when we will have to ask ourselves
what we spent our lives on and how life in general was better as
a result of it. On that day we will know the sanctifying value of
work.

Joan Chittister OSB

7

Cooking, cleaning, repairing, gardening, and farming – this is the
ordinary kind of work that is done in monasteries. Benedict calls
our involvement with such work an expression of love. Whenever
one of the monks tells me that I've prepared an especially good
breakfast on a particular Tuesday, I reply that I did it out of love.
Work should be done without grumbling, without sadness, and
without being overburdened. Help should be given to all who
need it. These are indeed fair employment practices!

Benet Tvedten OSB

8

When I studied medicine and something happened that I didn't
like, I could always say, 'Well, I will be out of this situation in a
while.' When I was in the Navy and found the life disagreeable, I
could always look forward to the day of my discharge, but when

I was in the novitiate of the Trappists, there was not such a way out. This time it was 'for keeps', and what was hard, unpleasant, or disagreeable had to be accepted and lived with as a way to purity of heart.

John Eudes Bamberger OCSO

9

We 100 Benedictine educators [at an International Conference on Benedictine Education] saw that the tradition we have inherited has more possibilities than we had imagined. First, we can structure our school timetables with greater attentiveness to that rhythm and balance which characterises the Rule. We can answer that modern cry of 'I'm too busy' by offering young people an induction into making time for what really matters, the life of the Spirit, not as a bolt-on option but as an integral part of the day. Secondly, we can keep alive that holistic sense of learning for which the Rule offers a framework, valuing knowledge for its own sake rather than for the exam results it brings, refusing to join the rush to make qualifications into commodities. In particular, we will want all our students to learn from the dispossessed, the poor guest in whom Benedict sees the person of Christ. Thirdly, we will use the new communications technologies wisely, seeing there an extension of the Benedictine tradition of learning. Finally, lay people will take increasing responsibility for managing schools, with a stable, praying community (of lay people and/or monks) to provide the essential foundation.

Christopher Jamison OSB

10

There is sometimes a temptation in the Christian life to pretend that all skills and gifts are things we should repress for the sake of God. We can dress this up in all sorts of ways, but in fact this is neither humility nor indeed Christian. Monasteries depend upon the skills of their members, and Benedict writes without hesitation that:

> If there are any in the community with gifts, they should use them. (RB 57)

It is of course part of the function of any leader, whether Abbot or anyone else, to call forth these skills from those around him. It would be quite false to the nature of a monastery for anyone to stand back, imagining that one is somehow serving God better by using nothing of what he has. Yet there is a hesitation in Benedict's mind which comes from the way in which the one who is skilled approaches his tasks. What Benedict wants to avoid at all costs is a sense in the mind of the monk that 'without me, this just wouldn't happen'.

Timothy Wright OSB

II

'Everything goes against the grain with me, the daily chores and my whole surroundings irk me beyond bearing. The length of the night office is a torment to me, I often collapse under the manual labour, the food sticks in my mouth, more bitter than wormwood, and the coarse clothing bites through skin and flesh to the very bone.'

A Cistercian monk

I2

A brother came to Abba Theodore and began to converse with him about things which he had never yet put into practice. So the old man said to him, 'You have not yet found a ship nor put your cargo aboard it and before you have sailed, you have already arrived at the city. Do the work first; then you will have the speed you are making now.'

Abba Theodore

13

If we wish to be nourished directly by the Scriptures without seeking a predigested substitute, then we will probably need to develop new skills.

The first requirement is patience. In fact, we have to slow down our intellectual metabolism and not expect to find quick and easy solutions to all life's problems. It is precisely this damping down of superficial excitement that creates the environment in which we are able to perceive spiritual things more intensely. It is like entering a cave. We need to give our eyes time to adjust to the dimmer light. In the same way, we who are so engrossed by the manifold concerns of daily living need to dull our surface sensibilities in order to become more aware of a level of reality that habitually evades our attention. Wanting to grasp everything immediately is the best way to comprehend nothing. We need time to adjust our rate of being to a more plodding pace and move slowly into a different ambience.

Michael Casey OCSO

14

'What usually happens to those not yet established in their chosen profession is this. They hear people talked about because of zeal or virtues which are different from their own. Straight away they want to take up a discipline like theirs, and because of human frailty their efforts are necessarily in vain. For it is quite impossible for one and the same person to shine outstandingly with all the virtues mentioned above. And if one tries to pursue them all together what happens of necessity is that in chasing them all one does not really catch any of them, and out of this changing about and this variety one draws loss rather than gain.

'The journey to God follows many routes. So let each person take to the end and with no turning back the way he first chose so that he may be perfect, no matter what his profession may be.'

John Cassian (Abba Nesteros speaking)

15

A hermit said, 'We do not make progress because we do not realize how much we can do. We lose interest in the work we have begun, and we want to be good without even trying.'

A Desert Father

16

Accidie depends on the con that life used to be – or will be, or could somewhere else be – better than it is here and now. Not so much melancholy as restlessness, *accidie* urges its victims to surf the World Wide Web of life in search of illusory fulfilment.

The risk in *accidie* is that one either abandons monastic life entirely or does so internally by escaping into fantasy as a protection from the demands of commitment or community. Anyone who has been married or has made a similar commitment to a person or a group knows the temptation. Early monastic writers urged hard work as a particularly apt remedy for *accidie*, joining work, of course, to a battery of reality therapies designed to counteract the allure of fantasy and self-deception. Work was not an escape from painful experiences but one aspect of healthy living. Work at that time was simple and manual, with clear and immediate results. The prescription of work as a cure for *accidie* is somewhat trickier today, when work is often neither simple nor immediately productive. Work can become an escape from *accidie* rather than a cure.

Columba Stewart OSB

17

Poemen also said this: Isidore, the presbyter in Scetis, once spoke to a group of monks and said, 'My brothers, isn't work the reason why we are here? But now I see that no work is done here. So I will take my cloak and go where there is work and so I shall find rest.'

Abba Isidore

18

When it is given to [a person] to know the overriding value of prayer as compared with any other activity, be it in the field of science, the arts, medicine or social or political work, it is not difficult to sacrifice material well-being for the sake of leisure to converse with God. It is a great privilege to be able to let one's mind dwell on the everlasting, which is above and beyond all the most splendid achievements of science, philosophy, the arts, and so on. At first the struggle to acquire this privilege may seem disproportionately hard; though in many cases known to me the pursuit of freedom for prayer became imperative.

Archimandrite Sophrony

19

St Benedict combined the Roman instinct for administration, a sense of law and order, with the saint's intuitive understanding for what Christianity is. Thus he is distinguished from some of the outstanding representatives of monasticism before and after his time: he relegated to a subordinate place asceticism and physical austerities. Benedict believed in the asceticism of hard and useful work. A Benedictine monastery is not a place where one goes chiefly to expiate one's sins, or because life 'in the world' has not been found worth living. Rather, a monastery is a 'school of the Lord's service', a place where one learns to be more fully a Christian.

Aelred Graham OSB

20

There are two poles pulling at the modern concept of work. One pole is workaholism; the other pole is pseudocontemplation.

The workaholic does not work to live. The workaholic lives to work. The motives are often confusing and sometimes even misleading. Some workaholics give their entire lives to work because they have learned in a pragmatic culture that what they do is the only value they have. Many workaholics don't work for work's sake at all; they work for money and more money and more money. Other workaholics work simply to avoid having to do anything else in life. Work is the shield that protects them from having to make conversation or spend time at home or broaden their social skills. Sometimes, ironically enough, work becomes the shield that enables people to get out of other work. As a result, although the workaholic often makes a very good contribution to society, it is often only at the expense of their fuller, wiser selves.

Joan Chittister OSB

21

Everyone from childhood upwards has to learn to take monotony if they would get anywhere. It seems an inescapable part of human existence, inescapable that is if we are true to our human condition. There must come a time for each responsible person when options are closed, a way of life is chosen and perseverance in that way of life will be the actual expression of our dedication to God. Perhaps earlier generations did not feel the same irksomeness in monotony; nowadays there seems a resentment against it as though it should not be, as though our interest and enjoyment must be catered for at every turn, and as if when work becomes boring we were justified in abandoning one field of action for another. All that matters is our fulfilment, our satisfaction in what we do and accomplish. We may call it other names but honesty should make us admit that we are crassly self-seeking ... No matter how much we enjoy our work, and surely this is desirable, there will be elements in it that test our endurance and patience over a long period.

... If we are looking for real heroism, the sort of heroism Jesus displayed, then we are likely to find it in some very ordinary man or woman, getting on with the job of living, totally unaware that they are doing anything remarkable and completely without pretension.

Ruth Burrows

22

Both the solitary hermitage and the coenobium [communal monastery] can be a trap. Solitude (eremitism) is not about spiritual elitism or preciousness. It is not the luxury of living alone, with great gaps of time to do one's work or enjoy one's woolgathering. Solitude can promote fierce and deep inner work – painful and sweaty toil, as the Desert Fathers and Mothers put it. They also called the monk's cell the 'furnace of Babylon'. Ascetical struggle, painful inner work towards true self-knowledge can, and should be a refining fire. Though such inner asceticism may be particularly occasioned by solitude, it can also happen in cenobitical life. Certainly a healthy coenobium ought to be able to provide time (and space) for deep reflection, long prayerful *lectio* [reading], and a place for peace of heart.

Donald Corcoran OSB CAM

23

Those striving completely to learn a craft make daily progress. It has to be so. But some know how they are progressing. Others, by divine providence, do not know. Now a good banker never lets an evening pass without his reckoning profit and loss. However, he can have no clear picture of this unless he makes hourly entries in his record books. For it is the hourly account that yields the daily account.

John Climacus

24

Our Lord said to his disciples, *See, I am sending you out like lambs among wolves.* Many, when they are put in a position of authority, are eager to tear their subordinates to pieces, showing only the alarming side of power, and hurting those they are called to serve. So eager are they to be in control that there is no love in their hearts, and they forget that they are called to nurture others. They turn from humility to pride and dominance, and if they sometimes stoop to flatter those around them they are full of rage inside. Our Lord says of them in another place that *they come to you in sheep's clothing, but inwardly they are ravenous wolves.*

Gregory the Great

25

A brother said to Pistamon, 'What am I to do? I am anxious when I sell what I make.' Pistamon replied, 'Sisois and others used to sell what they made. There is no harm in this. When you sell anything, say straight away the price of the goods. If you want to lower the price a little, you may and so you will find peace.' The brother said, 'I have enough for my needs from other sources, do you think I need worry about making things to sell?' Pistamon answered, 'However much you have, do not stop making things, do as much as you can, provided that your soul is at peace.'

Abba Pistamon

26

Christophe is the novice master and cantor and is also in charge of the monastery's substantial vegetable and fruit garden. The monks and a small group of their Muslim neighbours jointly run this market gardening enterprise. The work and the profits are shared. This co-operative venture with the villagers is a great source of companionship and spiritual strength for Christophe and the community. A small Christian island in the midst of a sea of Islam, the monks depend on the support and the goodwill of their Muslim neighbours for survival. And likewise the villagers find moral and material support in the presence of the monks at Tibhirine since 1938. This collaboration has become so close that a large empty room in the monastery has been handed over to the villagers as a temporary mosque while they await the eventual construction of a building of their own. Monastic office and Muslim worship thrive under the same roof while in the nearby town of Médéa violence and religious intolerance flourish.

Christophe Lebreton OCSO

27

Pseudocontemplatives ... see work as an obstacle to human development. They want to spend their hours lounging or drifting or gazing or 'processing.' They work only to sustain themselves and even then as little as possible. Pseudocontemplatives say that they are seeking God in mystery, but as a matter of fact they are actually missing the presence of God in the things that give meaning to life. The biggest shock of my early life in the community was to find out that novices were not permitted to go to chapel between the regular times for prayer. Were not permitted. Now what kind of a place was this? Here I was, set to get instant holiness and impress the novice mistress at the same time, but someone apparently had figured out both motives and moved to block the whole idea. In fact, they had something much better in mind for all of us. They wanted us to work ...

Genesis is very clear on the subject ... Even in an ideal world, it seems, God expected us to participate in the co-creation of the world.

Joan Chittister OSB

28

Some people when they build a house place bricks on top of rocks. Others raise columns up from the ground. Others still, when taking a walk, go slowly for a while, thus giving sinews and joints a warming up, and then stride out vigorously. Let the perceptive mind understand this analogy. Let us run our race eagerly as if summoned to it by our God and King. Our time is short. Let us not be found barren on the day of death and perish of hunger. Instead let us please the Lord as soldiers please the emperor; for at the end of the campaign we must give a good account of ourselves. We should be afraid of God in the way we fear wild beasts. I have seen men go out to plunder, having no fear of God but being brought up short somewhere at the sound of dogs, an effect that fear of God could not achieve in them.

John Climacus

29

See that you do not interfere in the affairs of others, nor even allow them to pass through your memory, for perhaps you will be unable to accomplish your own task.

John of the Cross

30

There is a widely accepted misconception among us that when one becomes involved in work at home or in business, immediately one steps out of the godly realm and away from God-pleasing activities. From this idea, it follows that once the desire to strive toward God germinates, and talk turns toward the spiritual life, then the idea inevitably surfaces: one must run from society, from the home – to the wilderness, to the forest.

Both premises are erroneous!

Homes and communities depend on concerns of daily life and society. These concerns are God-appointed obligations; fulfilling them is not a step toward the ungodly, but is a walking in the way of the Lord.

Theophan the Recluse

May

Balancing life

So let superiors take into account the weaknesses of the needy, and not the ill-will of the envious. But in all their decisions let them be mindful of the judgement of God.

Rule of Benedict, Chapter 55

I

A brother came to visit Abba Sylvanus at Mount Sinai. When he saw the brothers working hard, he said to the old man: Do not work for the food that perishes. For Mary has chosen the good part. Then the old man called his disciple: Zachary, give this brother a book and put him in an empty cell. Now, when it was three o'clock, the brother kept looking out the door, to see whether someone would come to call him for the meal. But nobody called him, so he got up, went to see the old man, and asked: Abba, didn't the brothers eat today? The old man said: Of course we did. Then he said: Why didn't you call me? The old man replied: You are a spiritual person and do not need that kind of food, but since we are earthly, we want to eat, and that's why we work. Indeed, you have chosen the good part, reading all day long, and not wanting to eat earthly food. When the brother heard this, he repented and said: Forgive me, Abba. Then the old man said to him: Mary certainly needed Martha, and it is really by Martha's help that Mary is praised.

Abba Sylvanus

2

Our basic problem with God is that we just do not trust him as we should. He who is infinite goodness deserves and requires our complete trust, but we do not always offer that kind of trust. We had rather have something a bit more concrete to hold on to, like that tough, self-imposed fast I just went through. 'Now that's something I know I did.' But I wonder whom you did it for?

David Altman OCSO

3

All we lack, now that life has become so speeded up, is the will to slow it down so that we can live a little while life goes by. We need to want to be human as well as efficient; to be loving as well as informed; to be caring as well as knowledgeable; to be happy as well as respected.

It's not easy.

Joan Chittister OSB

4

Something must be said about *the act of being pleased*. Suppose ... you carve out a chunk of leisure time and launch into a deliberate evening of relaxation. It may prove to be psychologically unnerving and emotionally disastrous, not because of any innate reluctance on your part; you may, in fact, be too much in earnest.

Most of us make the same mistake: we tackle our pleasure with the same blunt instruments we use at work. We have brought our hammers and nails, our ledgers, graphs, and measuring tapes, and applied them to the problems of delight. We are incurably attached to habits of the mind that are good for work but bad for play. Pleasure demands a detached and playful mind. It will not yield to command but only to surrender. There is no way to govern, master, or control it. Pleasure responds to wooing and wonder, not to aggression and manipulation.

William McNamara OCD

5

Leisure is not idleness or the pursuit of recreational activities. It is, above all, being attentive to the present moment, open to all its implications, living it to the full. This implies a certain looseness in lifestyle that allows heart and mind to drift away from time to time. Monastic life is not a matter of shoehorning the maximum number of good works into a day. It is more important that monks and nuns do a few things well, being present to the tasks they undertake, leaving room for recuperation and reflection, and expecting the unexpected. Leisure allows openness to the present. It is the opposite of being enslaved by the past or living in some hazy anticipation of a desirable future. Leisure means being free from anything that would impede, color, or subvert the perception of reality. Far from being the headlong pursuit of escapist activities and having fun, authentic leisure is a very serious matter because it is the product of an attentive and listening attitude to life.

Michael Casey OCSO

6

The monastery candles tell me day after day: time is going by, the light is waning, there are some kinds of uselessness that are essential. Then I have to make a choice. What is time for? If time is only for work, then what will be left of me when the work is gone? If there is no light in me, what will happen when darkness comes, as darkness will, to every life? What is the gain of leading a useful life if I do not also lead a meaningful life?

Abba Anthony knew what this culture must relearn: play and holy leisure are the things that make work possible, that make work worthwhile.

Joan Chittister OSB

7

Whatever it is – the soil, clay, wood, water, metal, cheese or chocolate, the monk needs this simple material to measure himself against, every day. He will thus be kept in contact with reality, for these things come from the hand of God and are solidly rooted in the earth from which they are drawn, and of which they remain a part.

André Louf ocso

8

The demon of *acedia* – also called the noonday demon – is the one that causes the most serious trouble of all. He presses his attack upon the monk about the fourth hour [10 a.m.] and besieges the soul until the eighth hour. First of all he makes it seem that the sun barely moves, if at all, and that the day is fifty hours long. Then he constrains the monk to look constantly out the windows, to walk outside the cell, to gaze carefully at the sun to determine how far it stands from the ninth hour [dinner time], to look now this way and now that to see if perhaps one of the brethren appears from his cell. Then too he instills in the heart of the monk a hatred for the place, a hatred for his very life itself, a hatred for manual labour. He leads him to reflect that charity has departed from among the brethren ... The demon drives him along to desire other sites where he can more easily procure life's necessities, more readily find work and make a real success of himself.

Evagrius Ponticus

9

All our good works consist in two things, namely in the active and the contemplative life. The active life is like wool clothing; the contemplative life is like linen clothing. The former is rougher, the latter more comfortable; the former exterior, the latter interior. The active life can indeed suffice against the coldness of

damnation and can wipe away all the shamefulness of sins; without the active life, the contemplative life cannot, in this mortal
domain, lead anyone to perfection.

Aelred of Rievaulx

IO

The theme of light and darkness in my life ... has been a constant
rhythm. At first I regarded darkness as a menacing chaos which
threatened to disintegrate me. The horror of a storm at sea when
I first crossed the Channel left me with an especial dread of that
devouring Mother. But I have now come to see darkness as that
primeval chaos over which the Spirit of God hovers, re-creating
me, bringing me to another birth. We have so many small deaths
to die. I value my time in darkness, my not knowing, even my
pain, as I then simply have to abandon myself to God. So my
prayer becomes a little more humble; I stop trying to organize
my own life and I rest in him. Often this self-abandonment comes
only when I have inwardly shed my tears of anger and limitation
and have accepted again that God is greater than I.

Paula Fairlie OSB

II

I don't think anyone can live contemplatively without discipline,
and that includes your local monk or nun. So, if I am going to live
as a contemplative in the suburbs, I am going to have to structure
my life, just as a monk or nun must structure his or her life. In
both cases, the structure, while it will be different in detail, must
be such that it provides regular nourishment for the contemplative dimension of life. This includes regular lectio, or spiritual
reading, to undergird it and to challenge the way I am living.

People living in the cities and suburbs, and in our society

generally, can make choices about the way they live, though most of them don't see that, because they are conditioned to be on the go all the time, usually at someone else's behest, from early in the morning till late at night.

Imagine for a moment what America would look like, imagine the degree of serenity we'd have, if laypeople had something comparable to the daily schedule of the cloistered life. It provides scheduled time for prayer, work, and recreation.

Joan Chittister osb

12

Prayerfulness of heart has much to do with finding the Center and then living out of that Center in everyday centeredness. Space and time for God are necessary for that centeredness that becomes [habitual] – the very baseline of one's personal melody in the Spirit. I once ventured to ask a markedly prayerful married woman how she prayed. She gave a surprising answer: 'I just putter.' She worked and accomplished tasks, but with a free interior heart – free for God, free for holy musings, and free for praying for others. Puttering is rather right-brained; it is not highly focused, not agenda-oriented, and not a charge up a mountain. Artists, poets, writers – creative and spiritual people – need non-agenda time in which to putter and live in 'interior space' where inspiration can happen. They need to cultivate the vessel of the heart: open, empty, and ready for inspiration – gift of the Spirit.

Donald Corcoran osb cam

13

The great spiritual teachers of all religions have themselves practiced and taught mindfulness.

To be mindful is to live in the present moment, not to be imprisoned in the past nor anticipating a future that may never happen.

When we are fully aware of the present, life is transformed and strain and stress disappear.

So much of modern life is a feverish anticipation of future activity and excitement. We have to learn to step back from this into the freedom and possibility of the present.

Bede Griffiths OSB

14

There is no commandment that says we have to be upset by the way other people treat us. The reason we are upset is because we have an emotional program that says, 'If someone is nasty to me, I cannot be happy or feel good about myself.' It is true that there is psychological and sometimes physical pain involved in not being treated as a human being. In such situations, we have every right to be indignant and to take steps to remedy them. But apart from such circumstances, instead of reacting compulsively and retaliating, we could enjoy our freedom as human beings and refuse to be upset.

Thomas Keating OCSO

15

Amma Syncletica said, 'There are many who live in the mountains and behave as if they were in the town, and they are wasting their time. It is possible to be a solitary in one's mind while living in a crowd, and it is possible for one who is a solitary to live in the crowd of his own thoughts.'

Amma Syncletica

16

In an era of hyperstimulation it can be difficult for people to realize that enlightenment comes not by increasing the level of excitement, but by moving more deeply into calm. There is a kind of monotony that is not boredom but paves the way for a more profound experience. Those who approach *lectio divina* in the hope of a fireworks display will usually be disappointed. Sacred reading is not merely a form of pious entertainment. Its aim is to confront us with the truth of our own existence, and to accomplish this it has to break down all the barriers that we interpose between our awareness and the truth. We have to move to a level that is different from the one on which we operate in everyday life.

Michael Casey OCSO

17

What lies behind each thing that I see now? Life is springing up and will veil some things even as others come to the fore ... It is an amazing rhythm. This is life. It is always moving, never still, always on the way, diminishing, coming back. And so I can think again clearly today about where and when and who I am. It is useful to take account of the fact that I am not everywhere, nor in some other place but only here. This is my limit. But I am at least here, and I am grateful.

Not only am I here, but I am here *now* ... That it is only *now* is another limit. It is only today, there will not be another. Stretch this fact out for a while and you have a lifetime. The *now* in which I am *here* is only a limited span ... I have only this day. It is given me. I may be given another or even many more, but one thing is certain: a day is not for ever and no amount of days ever could be.

Jeremy Driscoll OSB

18

We must never forget that, in spite of all our methods and all our efforts, we are and shall always be different from others. It is foolish to compare ourselves with others, and want to be like them. When we do that, we are doing the very thing that will make us apparently perfect, and yet perfectly inadequate.

I do beg of you: do not try to be above or below the golden mean. Try to be yourself, and to realize the fullness of your own life, without thinking that you are obliged to become a paragon of perfection.

A Carthusian

19

Almost everybody has at least one period of disintegration and disruption in their lives and it is a time of immense importance in our prayer journey simply because it is so difficult. We may be talking about an illness, a bereavement, prolonged physical pain, a breakdown or an attack of one sort or another, but every time, the primary characteristic of the experience is that it is imposed upon us, we do not choose it and would give a great deal, possibly everything, to avoid it. By that fact alone we feel robbed of our freedom, even plunged into the position of being victimised, at another's mercy, exploited. Sometimes we can see it coming, as when we know that a sick person will soon die, but even that does not prepare us for what happens to us when they do die. There is no preparation for this, which is why it is so searching, and when it comes we have no resources except the naked truth of ourselves. It is quite literally an *angustia*, a narrow place, in which we are straitened. I am in dire straits, we say, speaking the truth.

... Through it all, God works in our being, as we grapple with cosmic forces in the context of our small lives.

Frances Teresa OSC

20

A help toward a spirituality of busyness comes from Benedict's emphasis on interior disposition. He insists, for example, that outward obedience doesn't count if I obey with an ill will or grudgingly. In another place he encourages his followers, 'Let us stand to sing the psalms in such a way that our minds are in harmony with our voices.' The idea is that everything ultimately depends on my attitude and motivation. If I treat all my daily tasks (including housekeeping, parenting, and earning a salary) simply as challenges for me to master and control, then they easily become a source of tremendous stress. Everything changes, however, once I consider my busyness as a major way of loving my family, my way of using my God-given talents for building up the kingdom. I used to feel frazzled and pressured by the constant deadlines when doing our school's computerized scheduling and grades reporting. Then all of a sudden one day my responsibilities seemed much less of a burden to me: I had started to look at this job as my special way of loving 500 students. The pressure and the stress were still there, but no longer as the grim price exacted by my attempts at mastery. They had become simply an inconvenience that went along with my unique way of serving the kids.

Albert Holtz OSB

21

It is not the great religious gestures that matter. So many of us are prepared to die for God as martyrs. We imagine colossal, dramatic scenes where we make our final speech from the dock or to the firing squad. I suppose, depending on our temperament, we are prepared for that.

But what St Benedict asks of us is something much more demanding – just to live our everyday life with simple fidelity.

When it comes to the time of our meditation or Divine Office, we drop what we are doing and we go to it – simply. Not because

abandoning what we are doing is a great act of service, but because the worship of God and living our lives on the bedrock of
reality which is God, is of the supreme importance. Not to do it
would be stupidity. We need to be serious. Not solemn.

John Main OSB

22

Time is something entirely different in the monastic context from
that which a chronometer could measure. Time is not ours. When
T. S. Eliot says, 'Time, not our time,' he points toward true detachment from time. We claim to have time, gain time, save time; in
reality time does not belong to us. It is measured not by the clock,
but by when it is time. That is why bells are so important in a
monastery ...

There are occasions when it is time for something, whether you
like it or not. And if you come only five minutes late, the sun is
not going to re-rise for you; it is not going to re-set for you; and
noon is not going to come a little later because you turned the
clock back. Those are decisive moments, around which the whole
monastic day revolves – moments that the bell indicates, not just
arbitrary time of some timetable someone has made up. Let all
these bells which you will hear remind you that it is time, not our
time.

David Steindl-Rast OSB

23

Lebanon is indeed very much alive, a holy land in its own right.
The mystical experience of the dance, so different from our con-
ception of it, is described in the chapter on the Moslem Dervishes.
Far from being an exercise of rampant ecstatics or convulsives, it
is a real act of meditative prayer expressed in bodily movement.

The effect on both the performers and the onlookers is one of serenity and calm, though the dance itself becomes an activity of perpetually increasing speed, without however losing anything of its grace or tranquillity.

Aidan Byrne OCSO

24

On the one hand, your desires and feelings sigh for the narrow path that leads to God. But, on the other hand, you have a whole realm of worries about the people entrusted to you. The former is in light; the latter in shadow. Your own desires are in the brightest light and you regard them as house guests, but this worldly concern lies in shadows and you look on it as an intruder. You don't allow yourself to see that they belong together and this is why you so frequently experience depression in your spirit. For you fail to see your striving for God and your concern for your people as a unity. And yet they both can be bound together as one gain – whether you are sighing for heavenly things with great yearning, or whether you concern yourself in a godly way for the people.

Hildegard of Bingen

25

Today perhaps we are brought to the mountaintop; tomorrow we may be calling out from the depths. Today we look upon the Lord and radiant are our faces; tomorrow we may again have to call Darkness our friend. Today we luxuriate in the source of all life; tomorrow the hand of death may lie heavily upon us. Today we know why the Lord is mindful of us; tomorrow we may question why he even troubles to visit us. Today our joy cannot be contained; tomorrow our sorrow may be more than we can bear. Today we see how good it is for us to be here; tomorrow we may wonder with Job if it were better for us never to have been born. ...

Let us now ascend this mountain of God which his right hand has won, and ponder in his presence the seemingly conflicting truths in which is to be found our unending happiness.

David Holly OCSO

26

There is a small monastery in the high desert of California, located in the foot-hills of the San Gabriel Mountains. It was founded almost fifty years ago and has a community of twenty-three monks. Their ages range from 27 to 94. Its numbers vary as new monks enter in order to continue their search for God, and some monks leave, discouraged, despite their lifetime commitment, or become convinced a different life is more appropriate. In many ways it is archetypal of the broken and stumbling communities of modern religious who do not quite know themselves or their purpose. The Divine Office is sometimes sparsely attended or badly sung; private prayer is too often sacrificed in the regular and irregular busyness that somehow sweeps over monk and community. The monks too are looking in their own uncertain ways for God, or personal security, or an identity they cannot find, or safety that eludes them. They try to be honest with themselves, they try to lead a more authentic life, but even in the best of times that is never easy.

Aelred Niespolo OSB

27

In community, the monk learns to unify his life. In the world, a person can easily live in a series of parallel lives. There is for example the business man, the professional or the politician who keeps a complete separation between his professional life and his family life or between his professional life and his religious practice. For the monk, this should be impossible. A monk can indeed have responsibilities in his community and even outside the monastery; but all his activities form part of his monastic life, he does them as a monk. Otherwise the central element of a monk's being would be lacking, that is, simplicity, which consists in having one single goal, one single preoccupation in life.

... An authentic contemplative life does not consist in withdrawing from reality to live in an artificial or purely spiritual world. It consists in withdrawing to the center, to the heart of all reality. A healthy community life helps us to evaluate with serenity the varied information that we receive, the different events through which we live.

Armand Veilleux OCSO

28

Not all courses are suitable for all people. Each person should have confidence in his own disposition, because for many it is profitable to live in a community. And for others it is helpful to withdraw on their own. For just as some plants become more flourishing when they are in humid locations, while others are more stable in drier conditions, so also among humans, some flourish in the higher places, while others achieve salvation in the lower places.

Amma Syncletica

29

Because ... contemplative life requires and encourages the development of ego strength, monasteries tend to be populated by individuals who are very much themselves. This adds a certain 'spice' to community meetings and daily encounters. At times such seasoning can be too hot for some people's taste; they might be tempted to wish for something blander. But the resultant loss could be irreparable. This is especially true in an enclosed community, where homogenizing would diminish truth to a single dimension. What is needed is a love that welcomes people in all their uniqueness, that continues the dialogue till some understanding is reached, compromising on the specifics of planned action while refusing to split apart whenever the going gets rough.

Marie Beha OSC

30

Perfection, then, is clearly not achieved simply by being naked, by the lack of wealth or by the rejection of honours, unless there is also that love whose ingredients the apostle described and which is to be found solely in purity of heart. Not to be jealous, not to be puffed up, not to act heedlessly, not to seek what does not belong to one, not to rejoice over some injustice, not to plan evil – what is this and its like if not the continuous offering to God of a heart that is perfect and truly pure, a heart kept free of all disturbance?

A Carthusian

31

Hope and despair are not opposites. They are cut from the very same cloth, made from the very same material, shaped from the very same circumstances. Every life finds itself forced to choose one from the other, one day at a time, one circumstance after another. The sunflower, that plant which in shadow turns its head relentlessly toward the sun, is the patron saint of those in despair. When darkness descends on the soul, it is time, like the sunflower, to go looking for whatever good thing in life there is that can bring us comfort. Then we need music and hobbies and friends and fun and new thought – not alcohol and wild nights and immersion in the pain that is killing us. The worst thing is to dull rather than displace the pain with the kind of joy or comfort that makes us new. 'Give light,' Erasmus wrote, 'and the darkness will disappear of itself.'

Joan Chittister OSB

June

Talking money

As regards the price do not let the sin of avarice creep in, but always sell the goods a little more cheaply than do people outside the monastery, so that 'in all things God may be glorified'.

Rule of Benedict, Chapter 57

I

Divine love is not a feeling but a choice. It is to show mercy. The rich man, although he saw the beggar starving at his doorstep and could easily have reached out to him, just went on eating, drinking, and reading his *Wall Street Journal*.

Thomas Keating OCSO

2

An old man said: If you have lost gold or silver, you can find something in place of what you lost. However, if you lose time you cannot replace what you lost.

A Desert Father

3

What does the Rule of Benedict have to say ... to the problems of living a spiritual life in a materialistic world? How do we build community in a world that is immersed in itself? What, in other words, is Benedictine asceticism?

What makes the spiritual life different from any other life? What are we doing that is so different from what everybody else is doing? The answer is it is not what we are doing at all that makes the spiritual life different from the life lived without consciousness. The answer is it is what we are and how we do what we do that is the mark of the spiritual life.

Joan Chittister OSB

4

In the matter of money [Clare of Assisi] had a different approach
from Francis and saw no problem in it – or at least no new problem. While we do not know her mind for certain, we can make a
guess. She was so conscious of God's holy working in the world
... that she had no fear of the future. She never saw growth and
development as disasters but only as new areas of co-operation
with God. Money, 'that tainted thing', can symbolise what we
become if we surrender to avarice, or it can symbolise responsible
stewardship. Perhaps the power of money lies in this, that more
than most things, it reveals where we stand.

Frances Teresa OSC

5

Someone begged an old man to accept some money for his needs,
but he refused, saying that his manual work supplied all that was
necessary. When the other insisted that he should accept at least
enough for his essential needs, the old man replied, 'It would be
a double shame to accept it: for me to receive what I do not need,
and for you to give me what belongs to others.'

A Desert Father

6

Unless the monastery is one of those rare establishments that is
actually impoverished and has made strenuous efforts over the
years to remain so, monks and nuns scarcely feel the pinch of
poverty beyond artificial restrictions placed on expenditure.
Monasteries accumulate money fairly easily, sometimes because
of the generosity of donors, sometimes because of favorable tax-
ation status, but often through a combination of hard work and

frugal living. As a result there is no fundamental fear for the future, or even the sobriety that comes with having to skimp now in order to set by a little for later. Compared with so many exploited workers, recipients of welfare, chronic invalids, and those who are just unlucky, the monastic standard of living is comfortable enough.

Michael Casey OCSO

7

A brother asked an old man, 'Will you let me put two pieces of money aside in case I should be ill?' The old man replied, 'It is not good to keep more than is necessary for the body. If you keep these two pieces of money your hope will be placed in them, and if misfortune comes to you, God will no longer look after you.' Let us throw all our care on God, for he cares for us.

A Desert Father

8

'We see many who have given up very great wealth not only in terms of money but in land as well – and still they get very upset over a knife, a scraper, a needle, a pan. If they had kept their gaze unwaveringly on the goal of purity of heart they would never have got wrapped up in such trifling things and indeed would reject them in the same way that they have rejected lands and wealth. There are some people who guard a book so jealously that they can hardly bear to have anyone else touch it. Far from leading them to the prize of love and gentleness, this sort of thing becomes for them an occasion for impatience, even sometimes to the point of death. Out of love for Christ they have given away all their great possessions, and yet they cling to their old passion for things that have no importance, and even give way to anger because of such things ... One does not become perfect just by stripping naked, by being poor and despising honours, unless ... love ... is there, a love which is found only in the pure of heart.'

John Cassian (Abba Moses speaking)

9

Question. If I would like to give alms, but my thought has doubts about giving, what should I do?

Response by John

Examine yourself, and if you find that you are doing this out of stinginess, then give something even beyond what you should have given, for example an additional small amount, and you will receive God's mercy.

John (of Gaza)

10

Determining need is a matter of discernment rather than of absolute rules. Does 'need' mean bare necessity, or what is needed for me to grow and to flourish? Today we would incline more toward the latter approach than was done in earlier times. For us to discern genuine need, and to avoid misuse of things or of people, we have to learn how to confront our desires, which are many and often quite subtle, and then to surrender those which prevent us from loving God and neighbour. Desire in itself is good: it makes us get up and set about the search for God, fuelling the ascetical work of learning how to love. But we have an incredible knack for desiring the wrong things, or getting hung up in little desires while the great ones go unsatisfied. Confronting all of our desires, small and great, sick and healthy, is the only way to know what our needs truly are. Only then can our cravings become the basis of compassion toward ourselves and others.

Columba Stewart OSB

II

Question. If I settle an account and afterwards discover that I tricked my brother without wanting to, what should I do?

Response by John

If the amount is large, then return it to him. If it is small, then examine your thought carefully, asking – from the contrary perspective – what you would do if you were tricked by him and were about to receive that amount; if you find that you would indeed want to receive it, then you too should return it. If you would not receive it, then neither should you give it, unless the person was extremely poor; for in this case, a small amount would make a difference. In that case, you should give him what is fair.

John (of Gaza)

12

Jesus was elated over the poor widow who offered two copper coins [Mark 12.41–44]. ...Whatever we may give of all the things that belong to us – our money, our time, our magnanimity, our health, our thousand good qualities – even if we put all this at Jesus' disposal, still we are only giving from our abundance. And it will always remain hard and even painful for us to give from our poverty ... Happy are they who dare to give from their poverty: in the eyes of Jesus they have given everything they have.

André Louf OCSO

13

A brother asked Abba Poemen, 'An inheritance has been left me, what ought I to do?' The old man said to him, 'Go, come back in three days and I will tell you.' So he returned as it had been decided. Then the old man said, 'What shall I say to you, brother? If I tell you to give it to the church, they will make banquets with it; if I tell you to give it to your relations, you will not receive any profit from it; if I tell you to give it to the poor, you will not do it. Do as you like, it is none of my business.'

Abba Poemen

14

Poverty – the poverty of spirit of the Sermon on the Mount – is a total detachment from the material world. It is to recognize that everything comes from God – our bodies, our breath, our very existence. We cannot properly possess anything – not even our own bodies, as Benedict says. We can only receive everything from God at every moment – our life, our food, our clothing, our shelter, our books, our friends. Everything comes from God, created anew at every moment.

Bede Griffiths OSB

15

Not so much out of necessity has gold become enviable by people as that with it most of them can provide for their pleasures.

There are three reasons for the love of money: pleasure-seeking, vainglory, and lack of faith. And more serious than the other two is lack of faith.

The hedonist loves money because with it he lives in luxury;

the vain person because with it he can be praised; the person who lacks faith because he can hide it and keep it while in fear of hunger, or old age, or illness, or exile. He lays his hope on it rather than on God the maker and provider of the whole creation, even of the last and least of living things.

There are four kinds of people who acquire money, the three just mentioned and the financial administrator. Obviously only he acquires it for the right reason: so that he might never run short in relieving each one's need.

Maximus Confessor

16

It was said of [Abba Agathon] that, coming to the town one day to sell his wares, he encountered a sick traveller lying in the public place without anyone to look after him. The old man rented a cell and lived with him there, working with his hands to pay the rent and spending the rest of his money on the sick man's needs. He stayed there four months till the sick man was restored to health. Then he returned in peace to his cell.

Abba Agathon

17

Considerable attention – too much in fact – is being given to the project of six monks of Achel who are planning to form a new kind of group to live as contemplatives in the world and as wage earners, on the ground that the well-established business life of the big monastery is contrary to the monastic ideal and creates too much pressure ... The last thing they want is publicity anyway. It [the project] may in itself be a good idea. There is one ambiguity, if it is looked at in our American context. That now with automation the jobs are getting fewer and should a contemplative monk be taking a job that someone needs in order to support a family? The big question is – should a monk be a wage earner?

Thomas Merton

18

An important person came from abroad to Scetis bringing much gold with him, and he asked the priest to give some of it to the brothers. The priest said, 'The brothers do not need it', but as the other was very insistent, he put a basket filled with gold at the door of the church. The priest said, 'Let anyone who needs it take some.' But nobody came, and some did not even notice it was there. So the priest said to the visitor, 'God has seen your charity; go, and give it to the poor.' Greatly edified, the man went away.

A Desert Father

19

Our solitary life makes us non-competitive, at least individually, in an age of industrial technology ... Let us have the courage to accept being judged more or less as unprofitable at this level. Our real work is elsewhere ... The community, taken collectively, can, however, earn its living ... Traditionally, this has been done by having an industry managed by some of the monks, but in which the work is done in greater part by paid workers. Unless there is significant change in the Charterhouse, this still remains the formula which best suits its structure, and best assures a contemplative life to the community as such. But who knows what the Spirit has in reserve for our future? As for us, let us seek first the Kingdom of God, all the rest will be added unto us.

A Carthusian

20

It was said about one brother that when he had woven baskets and put handles on them, he heard a monk next door saying: What shall I do? The trader is coming but I don't have handles on my baskets! Then he took the handles off his own baskets and brought them to his neighbor, saying: Look, I have these left over. Why don't you put them on your baskets? And he made his brother's work complete, as there was need, leaving his own unfinished.

A Desert Father

21

The spiritual consequences of attachments ... need to be healed. The spiritual damage we receive from them usually lies in the subtle attractions of power without responsibility. We choose to be greedy, lustful and selfish because we like what these things bring us, but we give no thought (or no effective thought) to their consequences for ourselves or others. Because of the element of choice involved and because our will, as well as our woundedness, maintains our attachments, letting go of them can be like dying. For the attachment itself it is a dying, since it will have gathered psychic energy to itself and can seem almost to take on an existence of its own. When we make our first, feeble attempts at liberation, this energy will rear up to defend itself. To let it die is part of what Christ meant when he spoke about losing our life in order to save it. We must lose the things we fasten on to because we think them essential to our lives, so that we can save the true life which we live in God.

Frances Teresa OSC

22

There was one of the saints named Philagrius who dwelt in the desert of Jerusalem and worked laboriously to earn his own bread. While he was standing in the market place to sell his manual work, someone dropped a purse with a thousand pieces of money. The old man, finding it, stayed where he was, saying, 'Surely he who has lost it will come back.' He did come back weeping. Taking him aside privately, the old man gave it to him. But the other gripped him, wanting to give him a share. The old man would not agree to this at all and the other began to cry out, 'Come and see what the name of God has done.' The old man fled secretly and left the city in order not to be honoured.

Abba Philagrius

23

The man who thinks nothing of goods has freed himself from quarrels and disputes. But the lover of possessions will fight to the death for a needle.

John Climacus

24

Poverty, chastity and obedience – the renunciation of the world, the flesh and the ego – are the basis not only of all religious life but of all human life. Detachment is the universal law. You cannot enjoy anything until you have learned to be detached from it. It is not the drunkard who enjoys wine, or the glutton who enjoys food, or the sensualist who enjoys love.

Bede Griffiths OSB

25

Amma Syncletica also said, 'Those who have endured the labours and dangers of the sea and then amass material riches, even when they have gained much desire to gain yet more and they consider what they have at present as nothing and reach out for what they have not got. We, who have nothing of that which we desire, wish to acquire everything through the fear of God.'

Amma Syncletica

26

The [Carthusian] Order has had a long journey, from the little wooden hermitage in the time of Guigo to an institute of more than 200 Houses in the seventeenth and eighteenth centuries. Today we are a little remnant, like the Church in general, in fact. Like the Church in the West as well, we are tied to buildings that are exteriorly rather grandiose (but hardly adapted to the number of monks, nor to modern conditions of heating, electricity, etc.), which manifest less clearly, for the present-day world, the real poverty lived by the monks in their cells. It is true that this individual poverty has varied according to the standards of life in the world outside, but it is real, although subordinated to the contemplative life. It could be – but who can say? – that we could rediscover, in our own day, a way of life closer to the simplicity of those who began. Let us trust in the Spirit who blows where and when it will (John 3.8), and give thanks to divine Providence.

A Carthusian

27

A brother questioned Abba Poemen saying, 'Give me a word.' And he said to him, 'The Fathers put compunction as the beginning of every action.' The brother said again, 'Give me another word.' The old man replied, 'As far as you can, do some manual work so as to be able to give alms, for it is written that alms and faith purify from sin.' The brother said, 'What is faith?' The old man said, 'Faith is to live humbly and to give alms.'

Abba Poemen

28

Abba Theodore of Pherme had acquired three good books. He came to Abba Macarius and said to him, 'I have three excellent books from which I derive profit; the brethren also make use of them and derive profit from them. Tell me what I ought to do: keep them for my use and that of the brethren, or sell them and give the money to the poor?' The old man answered him in this way, 'Your actions are good; but it is best of all to possess nothing.' Hearing that, he went away and sold his books and gave the money for them to the poor.

Abba Theodore

29

The Hasidim tell the story of the visitor who went to see a very famous rabbi and was shocked at the sparsity, the bareness, the emptiness of his little one-room house. 'Why don't you have any furniture?' the visitor asked. 'Why don't you?' the rabbi said. 'Well, because I'm only passing through,' the visitor said. 'Well, so am I,' the rabbi answered.

On the journey to heaven, things tie us to the earth. We can't move to another city because we have a huge mortgage on the house in this one. We can't take care of a sick neighbor because we are too busy taking care of our own hedges. We go poor giving big parties in the hope for big promotions. We get beholden to the people who give big parties back. We take things and hoard things and give things to control our little worlds and the things wind up controlling us. They clutter our space; they crimp our hearts; they sour our souls. Benedict says that the answer is that we not allow ourselves to have anything beyond life's simple staples in the first place and that we not use things – not even the simplest things – to restrict the life of another by giving gifts that tie another person down. Benedictine simplicity, then, is not a deprivation. It frees us for all of life's surprises.

Joan Chittister OSB

30

Jesus himself speaks of desire, of love, but also of ambition, personal striving, and self-dispossession in terms of treasure. Here treasure is not simply what we possess; it is what we love, what we cherish, what captures the human heart. Our treasure, whether God, another person, pleasure, reputation, status, wealth is that which we trust, what we count on, where we place our security. The treasure is that for which we will sacrifice all other good, sell all, making it the pre-eminent value that has no equal in our lives. All human striving is directed, whether we recognize it or not, to finding this treasure.

Constance Fitzgerald OCD

July

Learning to listen

Listen carefully, my child, to the instructions of the teacher,
and incline the ear of your heart.

Rule of Benedict, Prologue

I

The preparation for listening to God is listening to others. The [Carthusian] Statutes insist on the quality of welcome we are to offer our brothers when we have occasion to converse with them or relate to them: we must know how to listen to them, and understand them with both heart and mind; we are to go beyond mere appearances, and not allow ourselves to be troubled by the different ways they may have of approaching the same questions. So the Statutes give us a whole pedagogy of what it means to listen. Listening to others is not the aim of our life, to be sure, but welcoming our neighbour in this way will train our hearts to become silent, in order to be ready to receive the secret of the Other. For, in whatever circumstances, our main concern must be not just to receive some message or other, but, through the message, to discover the depths of the heart of the one who is speaking to us. If we are not able to do this with the brothers we can see, how will we be able to do it with God whom we cannot see?

A Carthusian

2

To listen we have to open ourselves to someone else and let the speaker set the tone and the agenda. Listening puts us in a relationship with the speaker, and learning to listen to the scripture, rather than just to read it, is the best way to learn that God is talking through the human authors of the Bible. That makes a big difference to how we receive the word. It means learning to tune in to a different level of meaning. Since God is with us and his word is addressed to us, it means that we can respond to what we hear, not only as a piece of literature with our understanding but as a meeting point with God in prayer. Gradually, as we begin to understand a personal meaning in what we receive as God's word, we learn to turn our attention more to the speaker than to what he says. Here prayer expands to a simpler act of adoration of God.

David Foster OSB

3

Listen, always listen. Jo, an African economist, speaks of this in a new way. Listening, he says, is in Africa the function of the chief. Surrounded by others who help him to understand properly, he listens to each in turn. Then a direction becomes clear. Appearances notwithstanding, the head of a tribe often has a highly demanding life to live, since he is forced to listen to all.

Roger Schutz (Brother Roger)

4

When a soloist reads the second and fourth psalms at Vigils, we are obviously doing as the desert monks did before us. But even when we are chanting or reciting back and forth across the choir, we are listening to our brothers and sisters proclaiming the word of God to us! A visiting Zen abbot thought it strange that chanting psalms was the monk's main practice. One of our monks politely offered the counter view that our main communal practice was *listening* to the psalms. The pauses and silences are very important, very much a part of the entire prayer. In some sense, we only chant the psalms so we can be in silence afterwards and pray.

Cyprian Consiglio OSB CAM

5

'The heavens proclaim the glory of God,' the psalmist sings. But they do so without the noise of words: 'No speech, no word, no voice is heard'; yet 'their words [go forth] to the utmost bounds of the world.' A rainbow arches across the skies, quietly proclaiming the lesson of God's covenant with Noah. Still waters run deep, like the life-giving spring that gushed for Moses from a desert rock. The smooth rhythm of nature's unending cycle silently foreshadows the mystery of death that leads to life: 'Winter is now past ... The flowers appear on the earth ... The fig tree is forming its first figs ... and the blossoming vines give out their fragrance.' Wisdom enters the human heart without noise or turmoil: 'When peaceful silence lay over all ... down from the heavens, from the royal throne, leapt your all-powerful Word.'

James McCaffrey OCD

6

If the word *obsculta* [listen: first word of the Rule of Benedict] defines the overall action within monastic life, it is also a part of the message offered to a world that does everything it can in order not to listen. Listening takes place within silence, which is not simply a lack of words, but is a 'counter' to the noise of the world. True silence prevents empty words. One can only listen if one can hear. In the *otium* [leisure] grounded in silence, and in the 'sacred space' of the monastery itself, God not only speaks to the person, but as importantly, the person speaks with God.

Aelred Niespolo OSB

7

We must try to keep the mind in quietness. For if the eye is constantly shifting its gaze, one moment this way or that, then veering between upwards and down, it cannot see clearly what lies directly in front of it. It has to bring its gaze to bear on this object so as to see it clearly in focus. In the same way a mind distracted by thousands of worldly concerns cannot possibly bring a steady gaze to bear on the truth ... Another image: you cannot write on wax tablets unless everything previously written on them has been erased – and the soul cannot receive godly teaching without first clearing out of the way its own preconceived ideas. With this in view a time of withdrawal is of the greatest benefit, as it calms our compulsive passions and gives reason a clear space to cut them down to size.

Basil the Great

8

The practice of silence has its risks because silence is not always a value. There is an unhealthy and negative silence, a silence of death. Non-communication can express mute rebellion, obstinate refusal, deep resentment. By not speaking, one can often avoid being challenged, avoid taking a stand, avoid the relationship that may become too involving, avoid the demands of love ... Silence may be a sign of an underdeveloped personality, an introspective, suspicious, moody, morose, taciturn type of character. Or silence may indicate a vacuum of indifference and be the sign of a haughty, aloof disinterestedness. Such a silence is a closure, a selfish shutting-the-world-off, a withdrawal behind closed doors posted with a 'Do Not Disturb' sign.

Charles Cummings OCSO

9

Obedience is nothing else than the capacity to listen to the other. In awaking to otherness we hear the word within which we ourselves come to be. We know the mystery that is our life as one that is simultaneously the mystery of sameness and of uniqueness. But we stray from God when we lose this attentiveness and no amount of talking or thinking about God can truly substitute to this openness to him. We stray by drowning out his Word with our egotistical noisiness, the complex mirrorings of our imaginations. We stifle his life by our own self-fixation and by all manner of selfishness. The wise teaching of the Rule [of Benedict] is that we are invited to return to him by obediential attentiveness. We are to be listeners. The Latin root of 'obedience' is *ob-audire*, to hear, to listen. And the follower of Benedict is one who follows this teaching, committing himself or herself to the attitude and practice of listening, of attentiveness.

John Main OSB

10

Responsive listening is the form the Bible gives to our basic religious quest as human beings. This is the quest for a full human life. It is the quest for meaning for our happiness hinges not on good luck; it hinges on peace of heart ... By listening deeply to the message of any given moment I shall be able to tap the very Source of Meaning and to realize the unfolding meaning of my life.

To listen in this way means to listen with one's heart, with one's whole being. The heart stands for the center of our being at which we are truly 'together.' Together with ourselves, not split up into intellect, will, emotions, into mind and body. Together with all other creatures, for the heart is that realm where I am paradoxically not only most intimate myself but most intimately united with all. Together with God, the source of life, the life of my life, welling up in the heart. In order to listen with my heart, I must return again and again to my heart through a process of centering, through taking things to heart. Listening with my heart I will find meaning. For just as the eye perceives light and the ear sound, the heart is the organ for meaning.

David Steindl-Rast OSB

11

Surrender does not simply mean that I quit grieving what I do not have. It means that I surrender to new meanings and new circumstances, that I begin to think differently and to live somewhere that is totally elsewhere. I surrender to meanings I never cared to hear – or heard, maybe, but was not willing to understand. Try as I might to read more into someone's words than they ever really meant, I must surrender to the final truth: She did not love me. They do not want me. What I want is not possible. And, hardest to bear of all, all arguments to the contrary are useless. I surrender to the fact that what I lived for without thought of leaving, I have now lost. I surrender to the circumstances of life.

Joan Chittister OSB

12

We learned that we could bond with one another on some mystical level and as friends even as we felt at an impasse because of our disparate worldviews and lack of common concepts. At moments we glimpsed the abyss that divides our worlds and we groped for terms and concepts that both groups could relate to. At other moments, a profound resonance melted barriers. In all cases, an authenticity, a willingness to address the delicate issues of difference, a readiness to learn or to be at an impasse characterized the spirit of the gathering.

Jeanne Ranek OSB

13

The ammas [Desert Mothers] taught me to rethink asceticism. I shied away from what I mistakenly thought were the ascetical practices valued in Christianity. I came to see that God hands us our daily asceticism, if only we listen. Today my ascetical practices center on a heavy schedule of meetings: Am I centered, grounded, and ready to listen deeply? Do I prepare and come ready to share? And am I mindful and present to others? Choices around healthy eating and exercise, giving time to someone in need, turning off our radios, televisions, and videos, being truly present to family members, and choosing to do without more possessions are all contemporary ascetical practices.

Laura Swan OSB

14

Talkativeness is the throne of vainglory on which it loves to preen itself and show off. Talkativeness is a sign a ignorance, a doorway to slander, a leader of jesting, a servant of lies, the ruin of compunction, a summoner of despondency, a messenger of sleep, a dissipation of recollection, the end of vigilance, the cooling of zeal, the darkening of prayer.

Intelligent silence is the mother of prayer, freedom from bondage, custodian of zeal, a guard on our thoughts, a watch on our enemies, a prison of mourning, a friend of tears, a sure recollection of death, a painter of punishment, a concern with judgment, servant of anguish, foe of licence, a companion of stillness, the opponent of dogmatism, a growth of knowledge, a hand to shape contemplation, hidden progress, the secret journey upward. For those who recognize their sins have taken control of their tongue, while the chatterers have yet to discover themselves as they should.

John Climacus

15

When people ask how they can tell if they are making progress since they are not supposed to analyse or assess their actual periods of meditation, the answer if usually self-evident.

A greater rootedness in self, a deeper emotional stability, a greater capacity to centre in others and away from self are the signs of spiritual growth.

If you want to ask the question, 'Am I making progress?' do not look at your meditation. There is only one way we can judge our progress and that is by the quality of our love.

As the mantra leads us ever further from self-centredness we turn more generously to others and receive their support in return. Indeed, our love for others is the only truly Christian way of measuring our progress on the pilgrimage of prayer.

If we try to force the pace or to keep a constant self-conscious eye on our progress we are, if there is such a word, non-meditating because we are concentrating on ourselves, putting ourselves first, thinking about ourselves.

John Main OSB

16

A Cistercian monastery is a place of silence, a place where one can find the quiet to hear. A Cistercian monastery is a place of freedom, where all is ordered to free us so that we can listen and respond to the deepest aspiration of our being. Cistercian simplicity does not apply only to our striking architecture with its chaste unadorned beauty and our plainchant. Modest diet and a practical spartan wardrobe, along with freedom from radio and television and the distraction of travel and visits, all contribute to allowing the monk to cultivate through study, meditation, prayer, and work guided by obedience a mind and heart totally orientated toward God – in simplicity.

M. Basil Pennington OCSO

17

Those who cringe from silence see it like the plague, fearful of its weight, cautious of its emptiness and the shock that comes with its revelations. The heaviness and emptiness we feared give way very quickly to turmoil and internal pressure for change. Silence enables us to hear the cacophony inside ourselves. Being alone with ourselves makes for a demanding presence. We find very quickly that either we must change or we shall surely crumble under the weight of our own dissatisfaction with ourselves, under the awareness of what we could be but are not, under the impulse of what we want to be but have failed to become. Under the din is the raw material of the soul.

Joan Chittister OSB

18

Silence is the language spoken by solitude. Perhaps at first reckoning, we might consider silence merely the absence of sound. But silence is not something that begins only when sound ends. There is something awesome and breathtaking about real silence; it is numinous, pulling us out of our self-containment and calling us towards the invisible. Religious seekers 'home in' on silence as homing pigeons return to their roost, because therein lies the language for personal communication with the sacred.

Peter-Damian Belisle OSB CAM

19

When encountering a believer from another faith it is first necessary to take the trouble to understand that faith as far as possible. Next, we should try to find out what the other thinks of us.

Notice that this search for objectivity is already a whole spiritual attitude. It means acceptance of reality and humility before the truth. If there is lack of intellectual honesty, any manipulations of texts, or revision of history, particularly history common to both parties, dialogue becomes impossible. There is a close link between literalism and obscurantism. When there is no clear will to understanding it is difficult to get along together. Before accusing our literalist enquirers of bad faith we need to assess the possibilities open to them of access to objective historical facts.

Experience shows that those who make the effort genuinely to understand another faith or spirituality discover that their own convictions broaden, becoming less exclusive or dismissive.

When encountering sectarian or fanatical movements, it is important not to make value judgements about a faith, especially one we do not know. Better to keep a respectful silence.

Pierre-François de Béthune OSB

20

At first the practice of external silence may seem to increase the decibels of internal sound. But whatever appears as we become more quiet has always been there: the repetitious pattern of self-justification, the anxious review of what 'she said' and 'what I said,' the censuring of others' conduct, the circling of anger back over some presumed injustice. Something in us must enjoy sucking on the sour ball of our misery; at least it distracts from the question of personal responsibility.

How to still these destructive voices? This is the work of a lifetime. But we can begin by hearing the conflicting voices clamoring for our attention, listening to what they say, and accepting responsibility for answering appropriately.

Marie Beha OSC

21

Though I have been quite busy, I see more and more that the dimension of my life that has meaning is the solitary one, which cannot be expressed. There are things which can and must be communicated but it is an error to attach too much importance to them. I think it is really a waste of time for me to write more books on 'the spiritual life' in the usual sense of the word. I have done enough already. And at the same time it seems futile to write about the way the world is going: yet it is true there are times when one must speak. But one must be sure of the necessity.

Thomas Merton

22

A brother questioned a young monk, saying, 'Is it better to be silent or to speak?' The young man said to him, 'If the words are useless, leave them alone, but if they are good, give place to the good and speak. Furthermore, even if they are good, do not prolong speech, but terminate it quickly, and you will have peace, quiet, rest.'

A Desert Father

23

Ask my neighbor at home [a Muslim in Algeria]. In his eyes, who am I? Cistercian? Never heard of it! Trappist? Still less. Monk? Even the Arab word for it isn't part of his vocabulary. He doesn't even ask himself who I am. He knows. I am a rumi, a Christian. That's all. And in this generic identification there is something healthy and exacting ... You will see, too, that in his description, he will only be able to translate this reality according to his own religious points of reference: 'He prays, he believes in God, he keeps "Lent" and gives to the poor ... that's almost like us!' Thus, after being welcomed at several of our French monasteries, our young friend Mohammed said to me, 'You know, over there in France, I met some true Moslems!'

Christian de Chergé OCSO

24

There is exterior silence and interior silence. The monastery is, or should be, a place of at least relative silence in the sense of the absence of unnecessary noise and agitated movement. We are less assaulted by harsh sounds; rather we are soothed by the mostly harmonious sounds of nature, and bells and our Gregorian chant. This pacifies our sensibility and refines it. A heightened awareness is a common experience in solitude and affects all the senses, for they are all linked together. In silence we are more vividly aware of colour, and perfume and touch, because we are more present to ourselves. And little by little, we become attuned to the breathing spaces of silence between the sounds, as it were, like an underlying melody, not exactly 'heard', and yet somehow perceived, something that can take the character of a presence.

Silence begets an attitude of listening; a recollected capacity to receive the manifold communications of being through the doors

of the senses, which yet go beyond the sensual to become media-
tors of a communion of our mind and spirit with what is. The
artist, the philosopher, the praying person may perceive or, at
least, express in different words diverse aspects of this reality, but
all have need of silence, receptivity and awareness.

A Carthusian

25

Will purest silence
be found in the still, deep heart
of the greatest sound?

Michaela OSC

26

When the monastic makes a vow of stability it is a vow designed
to still the wandering heart. There comes a time in life when everyone else's family seems to have been better than my own. There
comes a moment when having everything seems to be the only
way to squeeze even a little out of life. There comes a day when
this job, this home, this town, this family all seem irritating and
deficient beyond the bearable. There comes a period in life when
I regret every major decision I've ever made. That is precisely
the time when the spirituality of stability offers its greatest gift.
Stability enables me to outlast the dark, cold places of life until
the thaw comes and I can see new life in this uninhabitable place
again. But for that to happen I must learn to wait through the
winters of my life.

Joan Chittister OSB

27

Recognising the Voice

'God is always at home. It is we who have gone out for a walk.'
(Meister Eckhart)

In the film
Dead Poets Society,
a student pretends
to get a phone call
during morning assembly.
When the phone rings,
he answers it
and tells the headmaster
that it is God calling.
I have spent
the majority of my life
waiting for that ring,
putting my life
on hold,
sitting through
sleepless nights
waiting, as if
for Godot,
but I only get
wrong numbers
or solicitors.
Each ring
I anticipate
a divine voice,
hoping beyond hope
that this time it is God,
but then it is
a lonely voice
or a distraught student,

and again
I missed God,
or did I.
I wonder if maybe
I have heard
from God,
but just haven't
recognised the voice.

Benedict Auer OSB

28

It is no bad sign when we lose the superabundance of pleasure we once had in lectio divina. It is a habitual indication that we have passed beyond the beginnings ...

Easy accessibility to God's word gives way to a 'famine of the word' (Amos 8:11–12) ... a chronic sense that we are drifting away from God and no longer able to hear the divine voice. False solutions present themselves readily. We are tempted to abandon our regular practice of sacred reading ... Alternatively, we may attempt to blast through the wall by will power and endurance; this way we eventually exhaust ourselves and the effect is equally uncreative. What is called for is a stolid perseverance while we are gradually changed ...

It is as though God is speaking to us in a new language. We need to sit quietly for a time and let the words flow over us. Soon some sense will begin to emerge from the confusion and new light will illumine the landscape of our hearts. We are being re-educated and our spirits are slowly being attuned to the subtle harmonies of God.

Michael Casey OCSO

29

The religion of our time, to be authentic, needs to be the kind that escapes practically all religious definition. Because there has been endless definition, endless verbalizing, and words have become gods. There are so many words that one cannot get to God as long as he is thought to be on the other side of the words. But when he is placed firmly beyond the other side of the words, the words multiply like flies and there is a great buzzing religion, very profitable, very holy, very spurious. One tries to escape it by acts of truth that fail. One's whole being must be an act for which there can be found no word. This is the primary meaning of faith. On this basis, other dimensions of belief can be made credible. Otherwise not. My whole being must be a yes and an amen and an exclamation that is not heard ... Utterance make sense only when it is spontaneous and free.

Thomas Merton

30

People are finding less silence in today's societies. They seek out places of refuge and retreat, hoping for the blessing of mere quiet and, perhaps, sheer silence. They go to monasteries and hermitages so they can learn to listen, or listen more attentively. Within monastic walls, silence is maintained so as not to disturb anyone who may be listening to the Word or simply resting the body. But listening is crucial there, and people recognise that fact instinctively. To what are monastics listening in their silence? To the word of God; to their inner-most hearts; to grace at work in the spirit; to what they discern to be truth – ultimate truth. Here is the place where one is ultimately completely naked – stripped of all pretension and illusion – and where one stands truly as one in the presence of God. Here one stands, simply and utterly, in truth.

Peter-Damian Belisle OSB Cam

31

A certain huntsman was fond of stalking the woods and fields for game. One day after he had been climbing up a steep hill for hours tracking his prey, exhausted, he sat down on a big stone to rest. Seeing a flight of birds soaring from one summit to another, he began to think: 'Why didn't God give me wings that I might fly?' Just then a humble hermit passed by, divined the huntsman's thought and said to him:

'There you are, sitting and saying to yourself that God has not given you wings; but if you had wings you would still be discontented and say: "My wings are feeble and I can't fly up to heaven with them, to see what it's like there." And were you then to be given wings strong enough to lift you to heaven you would still be dissatisfied and say: "I don't understand what goes on in heaven." And were you to be given understanding of this you would again be discontented, and say: "Why am I not an angel?" Were you to be turned into a cherubim you would say: "Why doesn't God let me rule over heaven?" and if it were given you to rule over heaven you would still be dissatisfied and, like another we all know, insolently seek something more. Therefore I tell you, humble yourself at all times, and be content with the gifts you are given. Then you will be living with God.'

Staretz Silouan

August

Working for justice

Listen well to what God says, for we are shown the way to God's
dwelling place: Those who walk blamelessly and are just in all their
doings; who speak truthfully from the heart and do not practise deceit;
who have done no wrong to their neighbours, nor listened to slanders
against them.

Rule of Benedict, Prologue

August

Working for Justice

I

Benedict reminds us that any person who yearns to draw close to God will act with justice. This includes both deeds of justice as well as a healthy relationship with others. Doing justice, especially when there is a price to be paid, opens the heart to hear the voice of the Holy One. The cost of justice may mean attending to our attachments, prejudices, self-will, or self-centeredness. For North Americans this cost is often economic, as we redistribute wealth to those in need. Just choices and actions literally move us toward the Holy One.

Laura Swan OSB

2

God, for us, is in this particular era with its advantages and disadvantages. Whether we like it or not we must live in our contemporary world and must love it precisely because it is God's will for us. We might well prefer the simpler forms of life of earlier days, we may fear and detest excessive technology, we may feel threatened and oppressed by what is going on and are powerless to prevent. I don't suppose our Lord enjoyed being in an occupied country at a time when the highest authority was not partial to Jews. I expect he too felt threatened. But we cannot opt out. We have to go on playing our part, or rather living our lives in this age, not trying to hang on to an age that has gone. To do that is to deny part of the human condition, and in the measure that we do it, we withdraw from Jesus, who embraced our condition as his *raison d'être*.

Ruth Burrows

3

It is in the desert that the soul most often receives its deepest inspiration. It was in the desert that God fashioned his People ... That is why the monastery is a kind of prophetic place, an anticipation of the world to come, a permanent declaration of a universe remade in God, a universe whose poles are charity and the praise of God.

André Louf OCSO

4

A world on the brink of marital breakdown, urban violence, international conflict, and global deterioration demonstrates without doubt that spirituality-as-usual has not worked. And no wonder. When traditional spirituality requires the invisibility of half the human race, the spiritual resources of the world go bankrupt. When spirituality means private piety, the public arena is left to develop devoid of the kind of values that give heart to the world at large. When spirituality does more to underwrite a system than to challenge it, the system eventually falls under the weight of its own decay. The social signs are clear: Something is missing from spirituality as we have known it because something is missing from life as we have designed it. Women have been left out of its conceptual development; men have been distorted and diminished by its assumptions; the world has been threatened by the hierarchal implications of its conclusions.

Joan Chittister OSB

5

We are a [Benedictine] community of hospitality. We create spaces in our heart and only then in our home and in our ministries for others. St. Benedict reminds us that in meeting the needs of the poor, Christ is 'more particularly' served. An important insight we have from liberation theology is that we do not presume to evangelize the poor or to bring Christ to them. Rather we go to the poor in order to find Christ and to know Christ better. Because of our prayer and our sensitivity to others, developed in sharing life in community, we are able to see the face of Jesus in ... the children, in the women on welfare, in the poor, the sick and abandoned. What we find as we work with them is not their conversion, but rather our own conversion.

Christine Vladimiroff OSB

6

An attitude of unconditional hospitality is always a religious experience, because it puts us in a position to transcend our limits and share in the creative caring of God. People are always limited, so this encounter is also a painful revelation of our limitations. We come up against frontiers, and not only language barriers but also irreconcilable incompatibilities.

Nevertheless we must always reach out to the other afresh, exposing ourselves to the unknown with the conviction that the God of the Exodus accompanies us through these difficult exchanges. The shock of meeting undeniable experiences of the Absolute, which are not yet possible to assimilate into our own experience, considerably broadens our religious understanding. *God is greater than our hearts* (1 John 3.20), and much greater than our theology. The little we know of God is based on a far wider fund of ignorance. So long as we remain in our traditional universe we can be unaware of this. But when we leave it, when we witness altogether different approaches to the Absolute, we can better appreciate how far God is beyond us and our contemplation acquires a much wider field.

Pierre-François de Béthune OSB

7

On the day the war [with Iraq] began, I lay down on the floor, flat on my back, to pray …

I feel in me a terrible something that I sense as vibrating through the whole world, as gripping billions of human hearts; namely, a sense that we are cut off from God and are left to our own worse instincts. But for the Christian such a thought must be considered a lie, the very conclusion desired by the Evil One who incites us to these wars. So, I am trying to battle against that thought. If the content of Christian faith and hope can vibrate in me, then maybe it can spread to the countless others who are also under the terrifying spell. Doing good – this will be my resistance to what the war has unleashed.

Jeremy Driscoll OSB

8

After days, months, of nonstop bombing, both in Afghanistan and in Iraq, we were apparently, somehow, waging war without victims. At great cost. With no public discussion of its internal implications for either country – and countries around the globe – other than the fact that we were hit and so we hit 'them' back. Worse, anyone who tried to discuss other dimensions of the situation was called 'unpatriotic.' Writers lost their jobs. Peace groups who pleaded for less barbaric means of conflict resolution in a world dangerous to itself were ridiculed. A terrible silence reigned. A fearful silence reigned.

The fact may be that we lose as much as we win in war. We lose our humanity, perhaps, because we have failed to contemplate that the river of pain that runs through the world cannot be staunched by force and the failure of reason.

Joan Chittister OSB

9

Abba James said: We do not want words alone, for there are too many words among people today. What we need is action, for that is what we are looking for, not words which do not bear fruit.

Abba James

10

Among christians and atheists alike, too much vital energy is used up in constructing abstract, ideal forms of society; at the end of it all, a lot of ideas but nothing is really achieved for humankind. Protest itself is now becoming another ideology, instead of being creative criticism.

I can see nothing more appalling than to live as an ideologist. Seek to free myself from ideologies – refuse the luxury of wasting the energies so much needed if the earth is to be made a place to live in.

Roger Schutz (Brother Roger)

11

So, my brothers, the community whose Superior spends his time travelling about dealing with secular affairs and what is foreign to his vocation and yet manages to force his subjects to keep to the regular life seems to me to resemble a handsome man who goes around with his head where his feet ought to be. I say this, although it would be no harm if we kept ourselves sometimes from passing judgment on the servant of another, or, better still, perhaps, if we shut up altogether.

Isaac of Stella

12

What is at the heart, the central core of the spirituality of inter-religious dialogue?

1. To search for God is to enter into a dialogue with his plan ...
   In order to approach this Mystery we need humility, receptivity, silence and a willingness to listen. We must hold ourselves ready to adapt our own schemes and to let ourselves be illuminated ...

2. Dialogue sends us back to the experience of God.
   To search for God in dialogue with other religious traditions helps us to understand the spiritual gifts spread out by God in the other religions ... we open ourselves to a God who is always bigger and, thus, truer.

3. A spirituality of interreligious dialogue depends on inter-relation, one of the most precious values of our time.

4. Today the search for God cannot live outside a context and cannot be either predetermined or isolated. For men and women of our time ... theories are not enough; they need life and experience. For this reason, questions about God take the form of a search that is experiential rather than intellectual.

Ramon Velasco OSB

13

I remember a conversation between [Starets Silouan] and a certain hermit who declared with evident satisfaction: 'God will punish all atheists. They will burn in everlasting fire.'
   Obviously upset, the Starets said: 'Tell me, supposing you went to paradise and there looked down and saw somebody burning in hell-fire – would you feel happy?'
   'It can't be helped. It would be their own fault,' said the hermit.

The Starets answered him with a sorrowful countenance. 'Love could not bear that,' he said. 'We must pray for all.'

Archimandrite Sophrony

14

There is an unspoken assumption in the *Sacrum Commercium* [a medieval Franciscan document] that private property has no place in Paradise, and it drops more than a hint that wealth is the result of greed and possessiveness. This notion has led Franciscans into a certain amount of trouble over the years, but the point becomes clearer when we reverse it and remember that generosity is a sign of Paradise restored. Francis and Clare, from very different backgrounds, both understood how wealth leads to more wealth in a self-perpetuating cycle of wealth, possessiveness, greed and aggression. Obviously there are some powerful social statements underlying the analysis of our Lady Poverty; perhaps the whole allegory should be required reading for those in public office. She makes some very challenging comments about the poorer people in a society, suggesting that the vitality of religion and the way we treat the poor are a thermometer for each other. When she, Lady Poverty, is rejected (and even more so when religion is either absent or just a pious front) then people will begin to snipe at the poor, seeing them as lazy, rough, uncultured and unfeeling, as being somehow to blame for their poverty.

Frances Teresa OSC

15

A brother questioned an old man, saying, 'Here are two brothers. One of them leads a solitary life for six days a week, giving himself much pain, and the other serves the sick. Whose work does God accept with the greatest favour?' The old man said, 'Even if the one who withdraws for six days were to hang himself up by his nostrils, he could not equal the one who serves the sick.'

A Desert Father

16

Three times daily the Benedictine Sisters of Idaho gather in their chapel to reflectively pray the Divine Office (Liturgy of the Hours). This formal prayer is a constant call to each sister to become immersed in scripture, particularly the Psalms. From this prayer flows the Benedictine commitment to justice and peace. In our various ministries and in our choice of lifestyle, we strive to promote the ideals of human dignity and the sacredness of all creation. Awareness of justice issues, both locally and globally, is an essential part of each sister's education and growth. When possible, sisters have been freed from salaried ministries to work directly with the marginalized.

Benedictine Sisters, Monastery of St Gertrude

17

If we are not aware of our own cultural biases and assumptions, we can fail to hear others because of the loud voices within. We need to enter into dialogue with confidence and trust. The conversation must be inclusive and yet we must allow differences to remain differences; we must not try to fix things up. Differences need not be perceived as threats. It is possible to listen and seek to understand their values, hopes, and fears; to stand in their shoes.
    ... The challenge is to maintain a stance of openness, vulnerability, and a willingness to stay with the conversation for as long as needed.

Laura Swan OSB

18

To become a slave to the pleasures of the table is to make the stomach one's god. Since our body, ever being emptied and drained, needs to be filled (and for this reason our appetite for nourishment is natural), right reason dictates as regards the use of food that we replenish by dry or moist nourishment, as the need may be, what has been used up in order to sustain animal life ... We should prefer by all means whatever is most easily procurable and not concern ourselves with costly fare and seek to obtain extravagant foods with expensive sauces ... On the contrary, we should choose whatever is easy to obtain in each region, cheap, and available for general consumption, and use only those imported foods that are necessary to sustain life, like olive oil and similar products. In addition, if something would be useful for the necessary relief of the sick, this, too, is permitted, if it can be procured without difficulty, disturbance, or distraction.

Basil the Great

19

As Christians and Benedictines we call for a return to the basic moral principles of our nation, principles of justice for all, hospitality to the oppressed and the immigrant, recognition and acceptance of legitimate differences, help for the poor, the deprived and the sick. We as a nation must know that the user of power is accountable to God, that might does not make right, that respect for all people is the duty of the civilized nations of this world.

As Christians and Benedictines we believe that 'Those who say, "I love God," and hate their brothers or sisters, are liars; for those who do not love a brother or sister whom they have seen, cannot love God whom they have not seen. The commandment we have from [God] is this: those who love God must love their brothers and sisters also' (1 John 4:20f).

Our brothers and sisters include all peoples, all races, all nations. If we are indeed pro-life, we must be for the lives of all the people of this earth. With Pope Paul VI in his address to the General Assembly of the United Nations, our cry from the heart is, 'No more war. War never again.'

From the Benedictine Peace Statement 2005

20

There is no hiding from struggle. It takes place deep down inside of us, in that tender place from which there is no refuge. No external enemy is nearly as demanding, as damaging, as destructive as the enemy within, the one of our own making. It is our own lust or pride or greed or jealousy or anger or gluttony or envy that takes us down. It is those against which we struggle. It is those that dog us from moment to moment, warring against the other forces within us, just as strong, just as intent, far more honorable. It is our innate compassion and humility and self-knowledge and largesse and justice and courage that call us to become our better selves. It is in the crucible of struggle that one of these outweighs the other, not always and not only, but often. In fact, is there anywhere other than struggle that they can really come to bloom?

Joan Chittister OSB

21

Inner stillness is necessary if we are to be in perfect control of our faculties and if we are to hear the voice of the Spirit speaking to us.

There can be no stillness without discipline, and the discipline of external silence can help us towards that inner tranquillity which is at the heart of authentic religious experience.

In meditation we take steps to achieve this stillness. We quieten our bodies and our emotions, then gradually allow the mind to become single-pointed.

Stillness within one individual can affect society beyond measure.

Bede Griffiths OSB

22

Thinking deeply of Santi Deva [eighth-century Buddhist monk] and my own need for discipline. What a fool I have been, in the literal and biblical sense of the word: thoughtless, impulsive, lazy, self-interested, yet alien to myself, untrue to myself, following the most stupid fantasies, guided by the most idiotic emotions and needs. Yes, I know, it is partly unavoidable. But I know too that in spite of all contradictions there is a center and a strength to which I *always* can have access if I really desire it. And the grace to desire it is surely there.

It would do no good to anyone if I just went around talking – no matter how articulately – in this condition. There is still so much to learn, so much deepening to be done, so much to surrender. My real business is something far different from simply giving out words and ideas and 'doing things' – even to help others. The best thing I can give to others is to liberate myself from the common delusions and be, for myself and for them, free. Then grace can work in and through me for everyone.

Thomas Merton

23

Romuald's love extended to those who did not always act lovingly towards him; for instance, he showed compassion and mercy to a thief the monks had discovered robbing a monastic cell:

The monks grabbed him and dragged him off to Romuald, who was waiting for them with a big smile on his face. They asked him, 'What do you want us to do with this guy? He is guilty of sacrilege.' Romuald answered, 'I really don't know. Should we poke out his eyes? But then he won't be able to see. Or cut off his hand? But then he won't be able to work and may even die of hunger. And if we hack off his foot he won't be able to walk. Anyway, take him inside and give him something to eat. Then we can decide what to do with him.' When the burglar had eaten, Saint Romuald, rejoicing in the Lord, gently corrected and admonished him with a few kind words and sent him on his way in peace.

Robert Hale OSB Cam

24

We Suffer from Ourselves. 'We may bolt the door but the thief is already inside.' The source of our suffering is often our critical, judgmental heart or a heart too filled with self-doubt to take its rightful place in life. Like a thief, we steal from ourselves when the heart is not grounded in humility. An attached, wilful, controlling heart creates inevitable suffering for oneself and for others ... Today, advertising is ever ready to advise us about the pleasure and comfort we owe ourselves. Persons who internalize pain like a silent suffering martyr inevitably give it release in acts of passive or active aggression or in codependent behavior. The inner thief might convince a woman to stay in an abusive relationship rather than take responsible action ... Women and men can be insensitive or indifferent toward the sufferings of others. The inner thief creates both personal and societal dysfunction through disruption of right relationships. We harm ourselves and others, through food, substance, or sex abuse. We harm the environment with poisons and pollutants, by litter, by misuse, and by overuse of our natural resources ... To be present to another's pain is difficult because it mirrors our own fragile hold on life.

The inner thief would have us deny feelings of fear and fragility in the face of suffering.

Vilma Seelaus O C D

25

Through the vow of poverty, we can enter into combat with the commodity form of our culture. In our day, I would define the vow of poverty as material, emotional, and spiritual identification with the materially poor. This identification is often called the 'preferential option for the poor,' for those who are *most* victimized, *most* enslaved, and *most* dehumanized by the rapacious greed of the commodity form. But we cannot prophetically denounce, we cannot be iconoclastic, we cannot shatter the idols of the commodity form if we ourselves are nothing but a celibate echo, a mirror of our materialistic society, of the commodity form, if we ourselves have become enslaved to the commodity. In that case, we are neither contemplatives nor prophets, for we are merely helping to legitimate dis-grace, the absence of the divine in our society.

Donald W. Buggert O CARM

26

More is gained in one hour from God's good things than in a whole lifetime from our own.

John of the Cross

27

The monastic community is not simply a place where we practice personal asceticism. It is a place where we seek the will of God together. Benedict wanted all the brethren to be called together whenever something important had to be discussed ... This is not a simple exercise of majority power, or of democracy before its time. It means that all should come together to listen to what the Holy Spirit is saying to each person for the good of all. Even if the abbot has the final responsibility to make a decision, the conventual chapter is the occasion for each person to exercise an act of community co-responsibility and thus to grow in the understanding of his own responsibility.

Armand Veilleux OCSO

28

Prayer made in common with believers of other religions is an experience which deeply transforms religious consciousness. It is a reversal of mentality which would have been unthinkable a few decades ago ... Monks and nuns who commit themselves to this dialogue at the level of prayer achieve an analogous change of consciousness. By praying not only *for* the whole human race, but also *with* those who pray in all religions, they discover both the specific character of Christianity and the universal nature of salvation. At the same time the image of the Church is changed, being positioned more concretely within the context of the humanity which surrounds it. The vocation to dialogue at depth is a service to the Church, but it is also a commitment to peace in the world.

Pierre-François de Béthune OSB

29

Letting-be is a way of living according to which we no longer view things, persons, or events in terms of their usefulness but accept them in their autonomy. We no longer wish to possess or subvert things to our own projects; we wish only to restore things to themselves and persons to their own freedom. In our lives as Carmelites, we should be witnesses of 'letting-be'. To the extent that we are, we are truly countercultural, for letting-be attacks the very roots of a culture hell-bent on possession, productivity, and domination.

Donald W. Buggert O Carm

30

Nothing can be offered to God more precious than good will. Good will means to experience fear for the adversities of another as if they were our own, to give thanks for a neighbour's prosperity as for our own advancement, to believe another's loss is our own, to count another's gain our own, to love a friend not in the world but in God, to bear even with an enemy by loving him, to do to no one what you do not wish to suffer yourself, to deny no one what you rightly desire for yourself, to choose to help a neighbour in need not only to the extent of your ability but even to assist him beyond your means.

Gregory the Great

31

We must enter into the world of the other, be he Christian or Muslim. In effect, if the 'other' does not exist as such, there is no space for true love. Let us be disturbed and enriched by the existence of the other. Let us remain open, sensitive to every voice that challenges us. Let us choose love, forgiveness and communion against every form of hatred, vengeance and violence. Let us believe without flinching in the deep desire for peace which resides in the depth of every human heart.

Bernardo Olivera OCSO

September

Opening our eyes

Since we have received a command to love God, we have been in possession of the innate capacity to love from the first moment of our being.

Basil, Long Rules 2

I

The whole universe is a sacrament, which mirrors the divine reality ... each created thing, though nothing in itself, is of infinite value and significance, because it is the sign of a mystery which is enshrined in the depths of its being ... Every human being is ... not merely an isolated individual carried along on the flux of time and doomed to extinction, but a member of a divine society, working out its destiny in space and time and subject to all the tragic consequences of subservience to the material world, but destined to transcend the limitations of time and space and mortality, and to enter into that fullness of life where there shall be 'neither mourning nor weeping nor pain any more.' The suffering of this world can have no meaning as long as we attempt to judge it in the light of this present time. We are like people who hear snatches of music, which they have no means of relating to the symphony as a whole. But when we have passed through the conditions of this present life we shall then have that integral knowledge in which the whole is known in every part, and every part is seen to mirror the whole.

Bede Griffiths OSB

2

Awareness puts us into contact with the universe. It mines every relationship, unmasks every event, every moment, for the meaning that is under the meaning of it. The question is not so much what is going on in the room, but what is happening to me because of it? What do I see here of God that I could not see otherwise? What is God demanding of my heart as a result of each event, each situation, each person in my life? Etty Hillesum,

Jewish prisoner in one of Hitler's concentration camps, saw the goodness in her German guards. That is contemplation, that is the willingness to see as God sees. It does not change the difficulty, the boredom, the evil of a pernicious, an insidious situation, perhaps, but it can change the texture of our own hearts, the quality of our responses, the depth of our own understandings. Without awareness, enemies stay forever only enemies and life is forever bland.

Joan Chittister OSB

3

My brother recently chided me for wasting days and nights in fruitless prayer and search for a dog lost in the woods. 'After all,' he said, 'it's just a dog, and you've got pressing things to do.' I've got to make him understand there's no such thing as *just a dog*. Every dog expresses uniquely the dogginess of God, a quality of God that can be found nowhere else. God is that dog lost in the woods. While he is lost, though I may not and need not find him, there is no other way for me to seek God here and now except by seeking the lost dog. The search cannot be fruitless nor the time wasted. The dog, lost or found, cannot be loved too much. Love may be spoiled by mawkish sentimentality or egotistic intrusions, spoiled precisely because of the diminution of love; but love itself has no excess.

William McNamara OCD

4

Seek in reading and you will find in meditation; knock in prayer and it will be opened to you in contemplation.

John of the Cross

5

When St. Theresa of Lisieux was looking back over her life she told how it was her father's custom, when she was a quite small child, to take her out before she went to bed to show her the stars. He told her the names of the planets, how they were grouped and how far away they were believed to be, and how everything in the sky was the work of God's hands. Reflecting in later life on these occasions she judges that they marked for her the beginning of her prayer life. She was not conscious of setting her mind to pray, and there was no set form to her prayer, but in retrospect she thinks that the majesty of God so impressed itself on her little-girl mind as to evoke a response which must have been prayer. Awe and wonder. The greatness of God. No preoccupations with the worthless self, no particular awareness that prayer is going on.

Hubert van Zeller OSB

6

At rock-bottom we are made in the image of God, and this stripping is very much like the cleaning of an ancient, beautiful wall painting, or of a painting by a great master that was painted over in the course of the centuries by tasteless people who had intruded upon the real beauty that had been created by the master. To begin with, the more we clean, the more things disappear, and it seems to us that we have created a mess where there was at least a certain amount of beauty; perhaps not much, but some beauty. And then we begin to discover the real beauty which the great master has put into his painting; we see the misery, then the mess in between, but at the same time we have a preview of the authentic beauty. And we discover that what we are is a poor person who needs God; but not God to fill the gap – God to be met.

Anthony Bloom

7

Another activity of the Spirit within us is looking. Looking gradually prepares us for seeing. 'The world will not see me, but you shall see me, because I live, and you shall live.' We see the Lord not according to the flesh, which is impossible, but with a vision in the Holy Spirit. We recognize Christ in things, in faces, and finally in the icon, the inner vision, that we carry in our hearts.

André Louf OCSO

8

Experience ... is not what happens to us, but what we do with what happens to us. Events and circumstances trigger reactions, but how we respond depends on us: the past of our biology along with previous experience, all summarized in present choices. No two people see the same thing or feel the same way about anything. This is a truism we all admit. But our own everyday experience so fills the screen of reality that nothing else seems real until we stumble over another's perception of the same 'fact' or come up against the hard rock of refractory reality. When this happens, we are offered the opportunity to go beyond naive subjectivism. We can open the window to let in a larger, more objective view. We are ready to learn. Since whatever lives is either growing or regressing, openness to change is crucial for realizing human potential.

Marie Beha OSC

9

When we look around at the world about us we see the earth, the sky, the water, the plants and trees, the animals and people. But what we have to do is to look behind all these phenomena

and discover their hidden source. Most people stop with the phenomena; they appreciate the earth or sky or flowers or the sun
or stars, they admire the beauty, but they do not try to find the
hidden source of the sky and flowers, of every single thing. We see
beyond only when we look with the eyes of the heart.

Bede Griffiths OSB

10

Standing on the shore and looking at the sea you can think of the
horizon as a meeting of the sky and sea in one of two ways. Either
it is simply a line running right and left, and denoting the limit
of your vision, or it is something beyond which other horizons
lie which in turn reveal other seas and lands and civilizations.
The latter view has no part of fantasy. What your perspective
tells you is provable fact. You may not be able to see beyond the
line of the horizon, but your knowledge of the physical nature of
the universe is adequate assurance of the facts and forms – that
they do exist. If you wish to inspect them for yourself you may do
so by travelling to them, but you do not need assurance of their
existence. The line of the horizon is an arbitrary demarcation, a
purely contingent affair, unlike the edge of a table or the drop of
a shutter.

  The acceptance of the world of the spirit can become a normal
way of looking at life – matter-of-fact as looking at television,
but with a new dimension added. Our knowledge of the spiritual
nature of the universe should tell us that our physical horizon is
not the only one, that the concreteness of things is not the entire
reality, and that it is the added dimension of the spiritual which
gives to the created order its total reality.

Hubert van Zeller OSB

11

I share the secret of the child, of the saints and sages, as well as of clowns and fools when I realize how wondrous and marvellous it is to carry fuel and draw water. Once the spiritual significance of such ordinary earthly acts dawns on me, I can skip the yoga and koans, the matras and novenas.

One finds pain and pleasure, ecstasy and enstasy, God and humanity in the commonplace. All these good natural experiences usher us, if we let them, into the presence of God, into supernatural life. It's better to stay home and smell a flower, bake an apple pie, or sweep a floor than to have a spooky, spurious religious experience at a prayer meeting. It's better to simply enjoy the sunshine or a good show than to meddle curiously and conceitedly with the occult. It's better to romp with the dogs in the backyard than rap with the intellectuals on campus or at church, if the dogs in the yard help us to be less egotistic and more God-centred.

William McNamara OCD

12

God cannot be just another of the things of this world, to be noticed also alongside all the rest. God's very being requires more than that, not *more* in the sense of quantity but in the sense of quality. And so, if God is here at all – and God must be because all the rest is – then it would have to be in the quality of something like 'between the lines' of things and persons, of something like the desire which others awaken in us but never satisfy, of something like a hidden radiance that we are longing to see, whose presence we sometimes suspect, but never see.

Jeremy Driscoll OSB

13

Entrance into prayer is an act of faith. By saying that, we mean not only that, when we think of God, we have to believe that he is, but we have to believe that he is everywhere, he is in everything, he is the origin and the source of everything, the end and the consummation to which all creatures are moving.

Praying is simply believing that we are living in the mystery of God, that we are encompassed by that mystery, that we are really plunged into and immersed in it – 'in him we live and move and have our being' (Acts 17.28) – that the mystery of God in all its fulness is both inside and outside us, within and without, like the air which surrounds us and penetrates into the tiniest hollows of our lungs.

Abhishiktananda (Henri le Saux OSB)

14

On one level [for the solitary], there is restriction of life: information, social contact, exchange of ideas, affective relationships, variety of interests, all these are deliberately lessened. To what purpose? Surely this represents a diminution, if not a frustration, or a mutilation.

This would be the case if such a restriction were imposed as upon a prisoner, or a hostage. But our solitaries do it willingly, they seek a great simplicity of life. Why? For wonder's sake. Wonder is a sentiment of surprised admiration, of joyful awe, of celebration and communion. And often it is the chink not too wide that lets in wonder. One tiny hidden flower and not the annual flower show with thousands of blossoms in pots. A simple blade of grass is enough if really seen with love and attention.

A Carthusian

15

To be made mindful, to be reminded, of what we know but have for all practical purposes forgotten is usually a greater need than fresh information. In this case the reminder is that *the Word has become flesh*. God is in us and all about us. No flight from the world is called for to discover him; no particular austerities; certainly no high degree of learning – only to cleanse our minds and open our eyes. The virtues? Granted faith and love, the qualities that are always in demand are best: honesty, courage, integrity, perseverance, directness, simplicity. 'Your every-day mind – that is the Way.'

Aelred Graham OSB

16

There was a time when I did not exist,
And thou hast created me;
I did not beseech thee for a wish,
And thou hast fulfilled it;
I had not come into the light,
And thou hast seen me;
I had not yet appeared,
And thou hast taken pity on me;
I had not invoked thee,
And thou hast taken care of me;
I did not raise my hand,
And thou hast looked at me;
I had not entreated thee,
And thou wast merciful to me;
I had not uttered a sound,
And thou hast heard me.

Gregory of Narek

17

It is interesting to note that in the primitive Christian literature, at least until the time of St Benedict, the expression 'lectio divina' always meant Holy Scripture itself and not a human activity undertaken with Scripture as its object. If one wants to translate this expression, it should be taken as 'divine lesson' and not 'divine reading'. Holy Scripture not only teaches the monk but transforms him in his daily contact with it. His whole life must be rooted in this lectio divina, this 'divine lesson', which he reads, examines, studies, interprets and meditates upon ceaselessly, without making any watertight separation between these different activities. If the monk lets himself be gradually permeated by Scripture, it will form him, gradually making him a true contemplative; that is to say, not necessarily someone who has what are called 'mystical' experiences, but a person who sees God in everything and looks upon everything in the light of God.

Armand Veilleux OCSO

18

A certain member of what was then considered the circle of the wise once approached the just Anthony [of Egypt] and asked him: 'How do you ever manage to carry on, Father, deprived as you are of the consolation of books?' His reply: 'My book, sir philosopher, is the nature of created things, and it is always at hand when I wish to read the words of God.'

Evagrius Ponticus

19

Before I had ever heard of the desert dwellers, I had entered into a desert season, not understanding that I was there nor why I

was there. I did not realize there was a purpose to my desert
sojourn. When I encountered the ammas [Desert Mothers], they
made sense of the desert in my life. Because our initial entrance
can be painful and confusing, we fear it and try to escape. We can
even fear our very sanity – until a wise one unpacks the potential
of the desert for us. The desert requires us to explore our crisis
of personal meaning. The ammas show us how the work of our
desert moves us through integration toward authenticity. The
fruit of the desert struggle is abundant life and deep abiding joy.

Laura Swan OSB

20

Simple impressions summarize whole decades of my life. A butter-
fly is my childhood. Green trees against the blue sky: the loneliness of my youth. Yellow dry grass: all of it together. I am walking in the orchard. It is Sunday. From somewhere low inside me
I feel my whole life surging up, decades of living and experiencing things; and the surge gathers into a capacity to see clearly
and to *be* clearly; and for some few minutes I am there walking,
completely alive, completely joined to the history I have lived, to
everyone who has crossed it, to all whom I have loved. But I am
joined as well to my future, which moment by moment comes
rolling toward me as I enter it step by step.

Jeremy Driscoll OSB

21

To one elderly sister who desperately claimed that God never
stirred the waters of her mind and heart, a pattern emerged clearly through her love of plants. Commenting on what these plants
she so lovingly tended in the chapel and along the corridors of
the convent meant to her, she enthused how some responded to

light while others shunned it, how a drop of her newly discovered plant food quickened life and brought forth broad glossy leaves and sometimes even blossoms in midwinter. What energy she brought to these descriptions! It was a short step from these observations to a stunned realization that these symbols of life and nourishment were the ways God had used to call her attention to his love for her. Walking around within the room of these experiences illumined sister's relieved acknowledgment that God was indeed speaking to her, calling to her, directing her.

Hilary Ottensmeyer OSB

22

We are apt to forget that to regard the things of the spirit as lofty and sublime is to put them at a distance, and so provide ourselves with an excuse for not attending to them. Religion might well be thought of as matter-of-factness, since it deals with the supreme Fact. But to see it so we need to be aware that God is not only 'in heaven', but within us and all about us. Our sense of God in his height needs as its complement a feeling for God in his fullness, a recognition that 'the world is charged with the grandeur of God'; and not only with his grandeur, but with his lowliness. For we are often nearer to reality when we stoop than when we aspire to the heights.

Aelred Graham OSB

23

Jesus, wrapped in the heavy clothing of Western theology, might well seem a rather foreign manifestation (albeit what in the West might be called *mythological*) more attuned with one's own culture in Krishna or Ram or the like ... This was brought home to me in a rather striking way, which was not without its humor.

Many Hindu temples expose a picture of Jesus for veneration as one of the manifestations of the Divine. A feast is celebrated in his honor on December 24th. At the puja service where rice and puri (puffy wheat flatbreads) might be offered to Krishna, I found the devout offering Jesus Pepsi, pizza, and potato chips.

M. Basil Pennington OCSO

24

[A monk from Illinois reflects on the differences of monastic life in a Guatemalan monastery]

The Third World experience forces us to face up to our fundamental vulnerability – both physical and spiritual. It is a personal vulnerability made more pronounced by the physical pervasiveness of everything from amoebas and parasites in the digestive system to the daily appeals of the poor made from sidewalk and roadside. It is a vulnerability shorn of the protective layers of community life in the First World where we are so accustomed to insulate ourselves from what we consider alien environments. In such a setting, headphones and compact discs are not only symbols of cultural shields; they stand no challenge to the sound trucks of traveling preachers and the pervasiveness of religious festivals.

... T. S. Eliot may have been right when he suggested that we need to portion our doses of reality, but from a distance it seems that a great deal of the Church's energy in the First World is given over to the disguising and reshaping of that reality, rather that accepting it as one more saving sign of the kingdom of God taking shape in the world.

Joel Rippinger OSB

25

One of [the Desert Fathers] followed by his disciples comes to the gates of Alexandria. He sees a very beautiful woman coming along the road. The disciples cover their heads with their cloaks so as not to fall into temptation. Perhaps they escape from the temptation of the flesh, but not from the temptation of curiosity. From underneath their cloaks they see their master and are scandalised to find that he is looking straight at the approaching woman. After she has gone into the town, they remove their cloaks and ask him, 'How could you succumb to the temptation to look at this woman?' He replied sadly, 'How impure are your hearts. You saw her only as a temptation. I saw her as one of God's wonders.'

Anthony Bloom

26

Obedience becomes hard when you have to be vulnerable to the other who has authority. You can play the obedience game in such a way that you never disobey any rule while keeping from your guide and director, your abbot or superior those things about which you do not want to hear a 'no'. You need a lot of trust to give yourself fully to someone else, certainly to someone to whom you owe obedience. Many people adapt very quickly but are not really obedient. They simply don't want to make waves and instead go along with the trend. That is not obedience. That is just adaptation.

John Eudes Bamberger OCSO

27

I hold a friend's hand in mine, and this gesture becomes a word, the meaning of which goes far beyond words. It makes demands on me. It is an implicit pledge. It calls for faithfulness and for sacrifice. But it is above all a celebration of friendship, a meaningful gesture that need not be justified by any practical purpose. It is as superfluous as all the ultimately important things in life. It is a word of God by which I live.

But a calamity is also a word of God when it hits me. While working for me, a young man, as dear to me as my own little brother, has an accident. Glass is shattered in his eyes, and I find him lying blindfolded in a hospital bed. What is God saying now? Together we grope, grapple, listen, strain to hear. Is this, too, a lifegiving word? When we can no longer make sense of a given situation, we have reached the crucial point. Now arises the challenge that calls for faith.

David Steindl-Rast OSB

28

Openness is the door through which wisdom travels and contemplation begins. It is the pinnacle from which we learn that the world is much bigger, much broader than ourselves, that there is truth out there that is different than our own. The voice of God within us is not the only voice of God. Openness is not gentility in the social arena. It is not polite listening to people with whom we inherently disagree. It is not political or civil or 'nice.' It is not even simple hospitality. It is the munificent abandonment of the mind to new ideas, new possibilities. Without an essential posture of openness, contemplation is not possible. God comes in every voice, behind every face, in every memory, deep in every struggle. To close off any of them is to close off the possibility of becoming new again ourselves. To be a contemplative it is necessary to throw open the arms of our lives, to take in daily one experience, one person, one new idea with which we have no familiarity and ask what it is saying to us about us. Then God, the Ultimate Reality, the Life beyond life can come to us in deep, in rending, new ways.

Joan Chittister OSB

29

The monastic night watch is good practice in the art of waiting, as we patiently look for the coming of dawn. Monks and nuns wait in the dark, longing for the light of dawn but unable to hasten its coming. No one can force the dawn or bring it about in any way. It dawns in its own good time on those who wait for it. The ability to wait is characteristic of those who have learned to slow down and live in the fullness of the present moment ... By quietly watching and praying through the night, I learn to live with the slow process of my own spiritual growth. I have no control over the future and I do not know exactly what will happen. I am asked only to stay awake and be ready because the light will surely come and will claim its victory over every form of darkness, despair, suffering, and death.

Charles Cummings OCSO

30

The Cistercian spirit of simplicity is engraved to this day on the very stones [of the Abbey] ... Beauty and simplicity preserve the spirit from distraction and lead it to God. Beauty leads to contemplation and is a sort of sacrament to the eternal beauty of God.

André Louf OCSO

October

Saving the planet

Let the cellarers show every care and concern for the sick, the children,
the guests, and the poor, knowing for certain that they will be held
accountable for all of them on the day of judgement.

Rule of Benedict, Chapter 31

1

Where there is no love, put love, and you will draw out love.

John of the Cross

2

Each religion has to undergo a death and resurrection – a death to its historical and cultural limitations and a resurrection to a new life in the Spirit, which would embody the traditions of the universal wisdom in a way which responds to the need of humanity today. No doubt we are all very far from realizing this unity, but as the different religions of the world meet today, we are discovering our common heritage and becoming aware of the unity which binds together the whole human race and makes it aware of its responsibility for the whole created universe. The concept of one world, one human race, and one religion based on the universal wisdom has acquired a new significance, as a way to escape from the disastrous conflicts which are dividing the world today.

Bede Griffiths OSB

3

In the coming millennium, religious leaders and spiritual teachers might consider as their primary responsibility not so much to convert new constituents or new followers to a particular form of meditation, but to create communion – harmony, understanding, and respect for everyone in the human family, especially the members of other religions.

In the world that lies ahead, religious pluralism is going to pene-
trate all cultures. How we live together with different points of
view is going to become more and more important. I don't know
whether we can make progress in such a project without a contemplative practice that alerts us to our own biases, prejudices,
and self-centered programs for happiness, especially when they
trample on other people's rights and needs.

Thomas Keating OCSO

4

The monastic community is home for us for a lifetime ... We
share life with one another and write together the history of our
community.

To the extent that I feel at home in my community, I can be myself, let my guard down, relax, drop the mask that I wear when
I want to make an impression on outsiders. Within our community each of us stands revealed before the others with all his or
her strengths and weaknesses, giftedness and poverty, confidence
and fears. Each of us is a mixture of splendid possibilities and
dismal limitations. Recognition of our basic human condition is
the condition for a full sharing of all life's joys and sorrows.

Charles Cummings OCSO

5

The ammas [Desert Mothers] model for us a way to engage the
concerns and pain of our world. Christianity is still wracked with
racism, anti-Semitism, poverty and greed, misuse of power, and
the marginalization of peoples. Yet there is a yearning for reconciliation, for a way to be found for Christianity to become fully
one in Christ. The ammas teach us that this prophetic transformation begins with our own interior transformation, and then

show us how to live out of that integrity. How do we let our spirituality influence our choices? ... How do we let people who are different from ourselves influence, inform, and teach us? Do we allow religious differences to divide us?

Laura Swan OSB

6

Imagine a world without forgiveness. What kind of response would we give to a hurt inflicted on us? Would we live a life of *tit for tat* and savor revenge for every slight we felt? Would we increase the distance between ourselves and others through avoidance and withdrawal? Would the cold silence of a frozen heart take the place of conversation? What barriers would we erect to isolate ourselves and our feelings from interaction with others?

Just contemplating a world without forgiveness fills me with horror. It would be the equivalent, in the soul, of the raging of war in the Middle East with no hope for resolution except death. There can be no real and lasting relationship if forgiveness is not sought nor offered as friendship develops.

Christine Vladimiroff OSB

7

We are all drawn inward, towards the centre of existence. We come to know ourselves as drawn into a presence. Solitude ushers us into presence, towards which the language of silence is most attentive. If we find ourselves in relation to that presence at the centre of our being, we will move our hearts, indeed our lives, outwardly in solidarity with all our brothers and sisters throughout the world, universally, without exception. The deeper the contemplative communion, the wider the embrace in solidarity. Solitude teaches us, after all, that we are really brothers and sisters of the same family. This is the great gift that the 'monk within' offers the world – human solidarity, universally expressed in communion with God. And a great irony rests within this gift. Authentically lived, monastic solitude breaks through human barriers of isolation and speaks a silent word of universal love and solidarity with all life.

Peter-Damian Belisle OSB Cam

8

We, the monks of New Camaldoli, are opposed to military action against Iraq.

As Americans become more conscious every day of sharing one world, one planet, and constituting one humanity with other peoples, we are confronted with a choice. Either we shall move forward toward an era of mutual understanding and unity, or back into a long age of national conflicts, which escalated to global magnitude during the last century. The proposed invasion of Iraq would be a major step backward into the world of violence.

We invite you to join us in prayer and action at this time ...

The coming of Christ, we believe, initiated a new age in the relations of human persons and of peoples, when rapacity and violence would give way to justice and peace. While it is obvious every day that the promised kingdom has not yet prevailed, we believe in the power of the gospel in this world and are committed to following the way that it teaches.

Benedictine monks of New Camaldoli

9

Slowly, painfully, we seek to allow the Spirit of God to renew the face of the earth. The restoration of society can only be achieved by those who are poor in spirit, gentle, compassionate, hungry for justice, merciful, pure in heart, and peacemakers. Only those who are part of the new creation can hope to build a new world, a better society. The kingdom of God is established first in our hearts. Unless that happens our efforts will remain generous and well-intentioned, but not the work of the Holy Spirit.

... It is our mission, throughout our lives to share the work of Christ and to renew, through the power of the Spirit, the face of the earth.

Basil Hume OSB

10

[Francis of Assisi's] affinity with all creation is in perfect harmony with the theology of the Christian East, which does not arbitrarily divide the world of animal and man, but strives to see the unity of all creation. The Feast of the Transfiguration clearly portrays this idea. Christ climbed to the top of Mount Tabor with three friends, Peter, James, and John. There, he was transfigured in bright light before them, and the whole mountain became radiant with that light. Christian thinkers in the East have interpreted this as a kind of call to all creation to rise to a new level of awareness. At the same time, Christ called each of us to change our behavior radically to meet this reality in our individual lives and circumstances.

The Monks of New Skete

11

In speaking for monks I am really speaking for a very strange kind of person, a marginal person, because the monk in the modern world is no longer an established person with an established place in society. We realize very keenly in America today that the monk is essentially outside of all establishments. He does not belong to

an establishment. He is a marginal person who withdraws deliberately to the margin of society with a view to deepening fundamental human experience. Consequently, as one of these strange
people, I speak to you as a representative of all marginal persons
who have done this kind of thing deliberately.

Thus I find myself representing perhaps hippies among you,
poets, people of this kind who are seeking in all sorts of ways and
have absolutely no established status whatever.

Thomas Merton

12

[One] role which monks and nuns might fulfill is to take responsibility for the short-term and long-term effects of human inter-
vention with the processes of nature and the fertility of the land.
Perhaps monks and nuns can be examples of the restrained and
prudent use of energy and alternative forms of energy. In an age
when people can scarcely think except in terms of the largest
possible scale, the fastest, most powerful, most up-to-date, most
expensive possibilities, monasteries might give witness to the
value of what is more manageable, poorer, more compatible with
the deeper needs of the human spirit. In a society where some
consider work merely a necessary evil and would prefer to live
on welfare or stock dividends, monks and nuns can be examples
of motivated workers finding a genuine fulfillment as human
beings.

Charles Cummings OCSO

13

There are probably billions of mosquitoes in any given season
around earth, and yet there are probably more stars. And when
you think of how much is going on in and around a star, even a

fairly average one like our sun, then to consider that there are more of these massive, complex stars than the endless parade of comparatively less complex tiny mosquitoes on any given summer night just in the one place where I am – well, then I ask, where on earth are we when we are in the universe?

Jeremy Driscoll osb

14

Without doubt, holiness is our greatest ecological contribution. Without it, we shall never balance the needs and rights of our diversified world. Holiness is restoration of order in its most searching and creative form, an unfailing source of respect for others. The reason why Francis is such an appropriate patron for ecological movements is not so much because he preached to the birds and rescued worms from the dangers of the road, but because he approached all that is made with a respect bordering on reverence.

Frances Teresa osc

15

Old men are naturally inclined to look rather towards the past, to relive and rehash the days of their youth. The Spirit, however, would turn their minds towards the future, a future defined by God's promises. He would have them dream dreams. There are of course dreams and dreams.

Some dreams are the voice of the past, our own past and that of the human race. Other dreams are intimations of the future; they cast a divinatory light on what is to come. And there are dreams that project what we desire, the state of things that we hope for. Some of these may be, in the popular expression, pipe-dreams, sheer trips of the imagination, which merely take the place of the real and its required effort and commitment. But there are others, the real dreams, that are like a star towards which we direct our energies, and these are rooted in real possibilities. They give form to the creative vitality within us.

A Carthusian

16

[Benedict] saw that the details and so the form of monastic life would be conditioned by the place and people that shape it. And it is precisely because of this insertion into its own time and place that a monastery has relevance in its social and cultural context. Because it is relevant it can relate to its contemporaries in contemporary terms, and because it can relate it can also serve. It serves by showing the society into which it is inserted that the ultimate meaning of men and women is found beyond themselves, beyond their culture and tradition. It does not do this by naively denouncing the secular – monks have passed through the same formative experiences in society as everyone else. It testifies by the way it arranges its priorities of living to show that the end of all our searching is only found by the way of transcendence. But its great Christian proclamation is that the seeds of the transcendent are planted in the soil of our humanity and our culture. Our spiritual journey does not call for a rupture with our humanity but the fulfillment of it, the natural continuation of it.

John Main OSB

17

In this feckless age of ours the senses need to be tuned and refined rather than mortified. How can you offer the world to God if you do not first take it in through the senses and make it your offering? Only a sensuous person can be 'obedient to the voice of Being'. In Martin Heidegger's striking phrase, 'Man is not the lord of what is. Man is the shepherd of Being.' How can we shepherd Being without a *sense of things*? We need to look at the world again with the eyes of a great delight, looking out gladly on the goodness of being. Matter matters before it means. 'The senses', as Heraclitus said, are only 'bad witnesses to those who have barbarian souls.' 'There is nothing profane here below,' insisted Teilhard de Chardin, 'for those who have eyes to see.'

William MacNamara OCD

18

Francis gave the brothers good, ecologically sound advice about the use of natural resources. He told them to leave a border around their gardens which had not been dug over, so that the grass and flowers might have somewhere to bloom and proclaim God's beauty. He used to insist that special places be set aside for herbs and flowering plants. He never wanted to terminate the life of anything and forbade the brothers to cut down the whole tree when they cut wood for the fire, because the tree, too, must be allowed the hope of sprouting again. This was not sentimentality but a deep and respectful awareness that nothing existed just for him, as if he were the owner in some way. Rather, he saw the dying and rising of Christ as the basic story, the foundation event of our planet, and possibly of the universe, and that everything which exists does so within these parameters. The trees, too, must be left with hope of their resurrection. Christ's story is our story and that of our planet, and by our lives, we re-tell it over and over again. We have no right to bring this story to closure in any of its myriad versions.

Frances Teresa OSC

19

The ecological crisis has created concern about the disappearance of entire species. For years I taught students at the Institute of Religious Formation at St. Louis University, a program that trained formation directors from around the world. Each year one met a panoply of charisms and traditions, members of ancient venerable orders and newly founded institutes, canons, friars, Daughters of Charity, social activists and hospitallers, monks and anti-monks (an interesting tension). It was a kind of spiritual zoo, a plethora of spiritual life forms, and a precious trove of experience in the Church. May they all not only survive, but also flourish!

Donald Corcoran OSB cam

20

More than ever, we realize our connectedness to each other, to the earth, and to the unfolding universe. Thomas Berry reminds us that we bear the universe in our beings just as the universe bears us in its being. The two have a total presence to each other and to that deeper mystery out of which both the universe and ourselves have emerged. A sixty-two-year-old business man describes this reality after cardiac arrest and a near-death experience:

> One thing I learned was that we are all part of one big, living universe. If we think we can hurt another person or another living thing without hurting ourselves we are sadly mistaken. I look at a forest or a flower or a bird now, and say, 'That is me, part of me.' We are connected with all things and if we send love along those connections, then we are happy.

Vilma Seelaus OCD

21

The hope of the future would seem to lie with the small communities ... which are springing up all over the world, consisting of men and women, married and single, seeking a new style of life which will be in harmony with nature and with the inner law of the Spirit. These communities cross all barriers of race and religion and are the expression of the urge to go beyond the present economic, political, and religious systems and to open a way to the future ... They can be likened to the monasteries of the Middle Ages, the centers of a ferment which would gradually transform society to make possible a new civilization.

Bede Griffiths OSB

22

The world is made up of events that are held together in relationship by unseen connections ... Relationships define structure, not the other way around. Living structures are constantly changing as the inner relationships change. They are a 'continuous dance of energy' (Fritjof Capra). Particles come and go, in time too brief to imagine, into a state of being through relationships with energy sources. Matter is manifested now as particles, now as waves of energy, always in relationship ... Even our observation of matter brings us into the relationship, into the dance, by which we are changed and matter is changed. Everything in nature is a web of connections, of potential relationships.

Ruth Fox OSB

23

The Lord bestows such grace on his chosen that they embrace the whole earth, the whole world, with their love, and their souls burn with longing that all should be saved and behold the glory of the Lord.

Blessed is the soul that loves her brother, for *our brother is our life.*

Staretz Silouan of Mount Athos

24

Are monks and hippies and poets relevant? No, we are deliberately irrelevant. We live with an ingrained irrelevance which is proper to every human being. The marginal man accepts the basic irrelevance of the human condition, and irrelevance which is manifested above all by the fact of death. The marginal person, the monk, the displaced person, the prisoner, all these people live in the presence of death, which calls into question the meaning of life. He struggles with the fact of death in himself, trying to seek something deeper than death, and the office of the monk or marginal person, the meditative person or the poet is to go beyond death even in this life, to go beyond the dichotomy of life and death and to be, therefore, a witness to life.

Thomas Merton

25

Deserting the human struggle in the name of the spiritual life belies the real nature of spirituality. The truly spiritual person faces every difficult question, every troublesome issue, every unresolved challenge squarely. Spirituality is not about specious consolations gained at the expense of full participation in the human race. It is about developing the courage, the determination, to commit ourselves to living all the dimensions of life with awareness and strength, with depth and quality.

There are issues in our time ... that need to be faced head on and subjected to the anvil of spirituality. The period is an avalanche of new ideas, disturbing changes, violent upheavals, and unresolved questions for which old answers do not satisfy. These very things are new grist for the spiritual mill. The temptation is to avoid the hard questions: to retreat to the past or to sit passively by, waiting for a clearer, calmer future. But that is not spirituality. That is comatose piety, at best. That is private devotion, not spiritual development, not the Christian life.

Joan Chittister OSB

26

We are a generation of seekers. We desire to know an authentic God. We want our faith to help us understand moral and ethical choices in work, education, economics, politics, and even our families. We want to integrate spirituality into every facet of our daily lives. We are questing for voices that have never been heard before. We are reclaiming women's spirituality and listening to the voices of nondominant cultures to help us find our way.

Laura Swan OSB

27

As Americans we are not educated for impasse, for the experience of human limitation and darkness that will not yield to hard work, studies, statistics, rational analysis, and well-planned programs. We stand helpless, confused, and guilty before the insurmountable problems of our world. We dare not let the full import of the impasse even come to complete consciousness. It is just too

painful and too destructive of national self-esteem. We cannot
bear to let ourselves be totally challenged by the poor, the elderly, the unemployed, refugees, the oppressed; by the unjust, un-
equal situation of women in a patriarchal, sexist culture; by those
tortured and imprisoned and murdered in the name of national
security; by the possibility of the destruction of humanity ...

We do not really believe that if we surrender these situations of
world impasse to contemplative prayer that new solutions, new
visions of peace and equality, will emerge in our world. We dare
not believe that a creative re-visioning of our world is possible ...
Death is involved here – a dying in order to see how to be and to
act on behalf of God in the world.

Constance FitzGerald OCD

28

Prayer is a heart that overflows with joy, thanksgiving, gratitude
and praise. It is the *abundance* of a heart that is truly awake.

One condition is therefore that our heart comes awake; for as
long as it remains asleep, our search for the organ of prayer in
ourselves will be in vain. We can try and come at it in various
ways; but the result will often be disconcerting. Some will put
most reliance on their imagination; but there is a considerable
risk of their ending up distracted and full of daydreams. Others
may try through their religious feeling, but soon get bogged down
in sentimentality. Yet others resort more to their intellect and try
to arrive at clearer insights; but their prayer remains arid and cold
and eventually ends up outside the sphere of their concrete living.
Imagination, feeling and intellect are not of the Evil One. But
they can only bear fruit when, much deeper within us, our heart
comes to awakening and they, fed by the flame of this spiritual
fire, themselves begin to glow.

André Louf OCSO

29

Our self-definition is that of a community of seekers. It takes fidelity and courage to persevere through the passage of time and the malaise of certain periods in our life. Our life is not a flight from the world around us as if to confirm a dualism that puts God outside the world. We live in relationship to our world, not over against but with and for and in criticism and compassion for the world of which we are a part. Our seeking puts us in the middle of those who search for a new, more humane society among ourselves, between all nations, and between human beings and the natural world of this planet.

Christine Vladimiroff OSB

30

Western monasticism ... is invited to break free of its cultural container to rediscover its inner identity and wellspring, and at the same time to discover a new relationship with everything around it: Church and world, humanity and cosmos. According to the mind of the [Second Vatican Council], this means to return to its authentic sources and to come into relationship with the movement of the Spirit in the world today – also in new, strange, and unfamiliar places and modalities. Put briefly, monasticism, if it is to bring forth a new wisdom, must open itself beyond itself. It must open to the length and breadth, the height and depth, of the gospel and Christ-mystery, of the human person, and of the experience of human persons in the world today.

Bruno Barnhart OSB Cam

31

There are two ways to live in the world – as if we were connected to it like a leaf to a tree or as if we are a universe unto ourselves. Obedience, faithful listening, is essential to the choice. A Benedictine sense of obedience is not designed to diminish a person. It is designed to connect us to the rest of the human race. If we have the discipline to curb our own caprice, we can develop the self-control it takes to listen to the wisdom of another when our own insights are limited. The fact is that there are few right ways to do a thing; there are only other ways of doing a thing. To be open to the way of those who have already gone the ground before us is potentially soul-saving. That is the function of Benedictine obedience and that is a tool of the spiritual art. It shows us in others ways to goodness that otherwise we might miss of ourselves.

Joan Chittister OSB

November

Giving and receiving

Since we are directed to love our neighbour as ourselves, we need to consider whether we have also received from the Lord the power to fulfil this commandment.

Basil, Long Rules 3

I

The 'love of our neighbour' – that outpouring of the love of God, or at least our striving to know what this means – leads us to see Christ in the guest who knocks at our doors, and in the poor, especially, who are in need of our help. The riches of the monastery, whether spiritual or material, are to be shared with others. A monastery may well appear to be a barrier – indeed, in a sense, it is symbolically so, for the values by which many people in the world live must not be the values of the monk – but the door must be open, and the porter welcoming.

Basil Hume OSB

2

The interdependence of gratefulness is truly mutual. The receiver of the gift depends on the giver. Obviously so. But the circle of gratefulness is incomplete until the giver of the gift becomes the receiver: a receiver of thanks. When we give thanks, we give something greater than the gift we received, whatever it was. The greatest gift one can give is thanksgiving. In giving gifts, we give what we can spare, but in giving thanks we give ourselves. One who says 'Thank you' to another really says, 'We belong together.' Giver and thanksgiver belong together. The bond that unites them frees them from alienation. Does our society suffer from so much alienation because we fail to cultivate gratefulness?

David Steindl-Rast OSB

3

In accordance with the counsels of Guigo, if a garment or something of that sort be sent as a gift to one of the monks by a friend
or relative, let it be given not to him but rather to someone else
lest it seem to belong to him. Hence let no member of the Order
claim a right of use or any other right in reference to books or to
anything else which the Order may have received thanks to him;
but if that use be granted him, let him receive it with gratitude
clearly understanding that it belongs not to him but to others. No
one is ever to have money under his control or in his possession.

The Carthusian Order

4

The one who reveals himself as friend acts as he who considers
my life worth the price of at least some of his own. This is the
secret of his attraction. A person who makes a habit of giving bits
of his own life so that this one or that may have more life, acts as
a strong magnet to every man, woman and child who is in need.
Animals also come to such a one mutely asking to have their lack
made good. Even limited willingness or ability to give life in any
form attracts a crowd of needy, and around those who set no
limits there is so dense a crowd that all of their life risks being
suffocated out of them. Although the crowd is a crowd of needy,
of those who are inadequate and in search of what they lack, yet
because in this life-giver they find just that, it is a festive crowd.
Round this person there will be laughter and an atmosphere of
celebration. He is in truth the life and soul of the party; for the
party is a celebration of this his life, available as so many presents
given away.

Virginia Cuthbert (V. M. Carver) cscl

5

Among other evidences of holy life, Aidan gave ... an inspiring example of self-discipline and continence, and the highest recommendation of his teaching to all was that he and his followers lived as they taught. He never sought or cared for any worldly possessions, and loved to give away to the poor whatever he received from kings or wealthy folk. Whether in town or country, he always travelled on foot unless compelled by necessity to ride, and whenever he met anyone, whether high or low, he stopped and spoke to them.

Bede

6

Simplicity is more than the key to personal freedom. Simplicity is also the basis of human community. Common ownership and personal dependence are the foundations of mutual respect. If I know that I literally cannot exist without you, without your work, without your support ... without your help, as is true in any community life, then I cannot bury myself away where you and your life are unimportant to me. I cannot fail to meet your needs, as you have met my needs, when the dearth in you appeals for the gifts in me. It is my ability to respond to your needs, in fact, that is my claim, my guarantee, of your presence in my own life. In community life, we genuinely need one another. We rely on one another. Community life is based on mutual giving.

The family, the relationship that attempts to reconcile the idea of community with the independent and the independently wealthy, the perfectly, the totally, the smugly self-sufficient, is no community, no family, no relationship at all.

Joan Chittister OSB

7

Spiritual maturity shows itself in the ability to transcend not only repeated frustrations but the mood of despair which repeated frustrations can engender. The spiritually mature are not impervious to disappointment, but are perhaps more keenly sensitive to it than most. The point is that they are not governed by it, do not sink into self-pity because of it, are not fatalistic about it. They accept the cross and even, without being morbid or superstitious about it, expect the cross; they do not make it their whole preoccupation ... In any age when achievement counts far more than motive, efficiency is often mistaken for maturity.

Achievement is not the lot of all, so the Christian would be wise to cultivate the disposition of being content to do with out.

Hubert van Zeller osb

8

Avoid being bashful with God, as some people are, in the belief that they are being humble. It would not be humility on your part if the King were to do you a favour and you refused to accept it; but you would be showing humility by taking it, and being pleased with it, yet realizing how far you are from deserving it. A fine humility it would be if I had the Emperor of heaven and earth in my house, coming to it to do me a favour and to delight in my company, and I were so humble that I would not answer his questions, nor remain with him, nor accept what he gave me, but left him alone. Or if he were to speak to me and beg me to ask for what I wanted, and I were so humble that I preferred to remain poor and even let him go away, so that he could see I had not sufficient resolution.

Have nothing to do with that kind of humility.

Teresa of Avila

9

That long journey round the world [to Australia and Japan to talk to religious communities there] points up for me the paradox, the surprising quality of God's dealings with us. One enters an enclosed monastery, through the 'narrow gate', only to find oneself years later being sent round the world, to 'the lands of sunrise and sunset'; one 'gives up' so much at the human level, and it is poured back: a fullness of life, wide horizons and the gift of undreamed friendships. I never experience this outgoing activity as in any sense conflicting or competing with the inwardness and silence. The word that is spoken is the word that has first been listened to; if not, it will be only 'sound and fury, signifying nothing'. The inwardness seems to demand the communication, and vice versa. This gives rise to reflections on the meaning of 'contemplative monastic life': I wonder, for instance, whether it is not more threatened by excessive human isolation than by excessive human contact, in the case of some enclosed nuns.

Maria Boulding OSB

10

Monastic spirituality teaches us that we are on a journey. The journey is inward to seek God in prayer and silence. Taken alone we can romanticize this aspect of our life. We can desire to pitch our tent on Mount Tabor and sit with God. We can use the monastery, the Mount, as a nest. But to be monastic there is a parallel journey – the journey outward. We live in community to grow in sensitivity to the needs of others. The only competition allowed is to outstrip each other in showing love and respect. The monastery is then a center to come out of and to invite others into. The key is always to maintain both journeys – inward and outward.

Christine Vladimiroff OSB

11

Father Daniel, at the age of ninety, was on his way to the front door for a walk one Sunday afternoon. Passing through the lobby, he came upon a young man and his mother. No one was attending to them, and Father Dan exclaimed, 'Oh hell! Now I've got to do hospitality.' Despite his initial reaction and response, he did the right thing. He took them downstairs and gave them cookies and coffee.

Benet Tvedten OSB

12

Holiness does not lie on the other side of temptation; it is to be found in the midst of temptation. It does not sit waiting for us on a level above our weakness; it is given us in weakness, or else we would elude the power of God that is operative only in our weakness. Rather we must learn to 'abide' in weakness, and to do so full of faith, open to the weakness and in utter surrender to God's mercy. It is only in our weakness that we are vulnerable to his love and power. Accordingly, to continue in the situation of temptation and weakness is the only way for us to connect with grace, the only way we can become miracles of God's mercy.

André Louf OCSO

13

The kind of life that I represent is a life that is openness to gift; gift from God and gift from others.

It is not that we go out into the world with a capacity to love others greatly. This too we know in ourselves, that our capacity for love is limited. And it has to be completed with the capacity to be loved, to accept love from others, to want to be loved by others, to admit our loneliness and to live with our loneliness because everybody is lonely ... The monk in his solitude and in his meditation seeks this dimension of life.

Thomas Merton

14

We have in hospitality a fundamental religious practice concerned with strangers. It is an ideal model for encounter with believers from another religion.

Until quite recently the practice of hospitality did not take much account of the guest's religion ... But things are different today. We regularly come into contact with people of other religions. If we want to show them respect, the religion of the guest must also be respected in how we receive them.

Welcome of a stranger is made possible by a common *humanitas*. Human nature is essentially religious. So, when receiving a guest belonging to another religion, that religion is not to be ignored. If the guest is considered a messenger from God, this must equally be so whatever his religious affiliation. Meeting a representative of another religion in a spiritual environment can be a stimulus to our own faith. God has indeed something to say to us by means of men and women of other religions.

Pierre-François de Béthune OSB

15

'Why does a woman like you stay in the church?' a woman asked from the depths of a dark audience years ago. 'Because,' I answered, 'every time I thought about leaving, I found myself thinking of oysters.' 'Oysters?' she said. 'What do oysters have to do with it?' 'Well,' I answered her in the darkness of the huge auditorium, 'I realized that an oyster is an organism that defends itself by excreting a substance to protect itself against the sand of its spawning bed. The more sand in the oyster, the more chemical the oyster produces until finally, after layer upon layer of gel, the sand turns into a pearl. And the oyster itself becomes more valuable in the process. At that moment, I discovered the ministry of irritation.'

I stay in the church with all my challenge and despite its resistance, knowing that before this is over, both it and I will have become what we have the capacity to be – followers of the Christ who listened to women, taught them theology, and raised them from the dead.

Joan Chittister OSB

16

The ultimate mystery cannot be named, cannot be properly conceived.

This is the foundation of all theology, this understanding that the ultimate mystery of being, by whatever name it is known, cannot be properly named or conceived. All words which are used about this mystery are signs or symbols of the ineffable and are of value only in so far as they point towards this mystery and enable its presence to be experienced in the 'heart' or the inner 'centre' of the person beyond speech and thought.

This presence cannot be known by the senses or by the rational mind. It is unseen but seeing; unheard but hearing; unperceived but perceiving; unknown but knowing.

Bede Griffiths OSB

17

Life is give-and-take, not give or take. Spasmodic gasping is one thing, healthy breathing another. When we take a hearty breath, we give ourselves to the air we inhale; and when we give it out again, we take a quick break from breathing. This balance of giving and taking is a key to healthy living on every level of life. In fact, balance is too mechanical a word to apply to the intimate intricacy of this give-and-take. We are talking about a giving within taking and a taking within giving. Once this is spelled out, it is hardly necessary to stress the fact that we are not playing off giving against taking. By no means. We are playing off a life-giving give-and-take against a mere taking that is as deadly as a mere giving. It matters little whether you merely take a breath and stop, or give a breath and stop there. In either case, you're dead.

David Steindl-Rast OSB

18

Question. Since every food contains a natural sweetness, is this spiritually harmful to the person who eats it?

Response by John
God our Master created this sweetness in each food, and there is no harm in eating of this with thanksgiving. However, one should always guard against attachment; for this is what is harmful to the soul.

John (of Gaza)

19

A spark plug works only when there's a gap between two elements. An electrical charge is sent to the spark plug, creating a spark in that gap, which in turn explodes the gasoline in the cylinder and powers the engine. All the action is in the gap. A saint's life is similar: holiness is like the spark that happens in the gap between the actual and the ideal, in the realm of striving, struggling, and thirsting for God. Without that distance to be overcome, there can be no holiness.

Albert Holtz OSB

20

When we try to get a picture of [St] Clare's life as a whole, we see that it has an oscillating, twofold movement which, on further thought, we may recognise. Her energy runs outward to action and inward to reflection, each part of the movement drawing on the previous one and preparing for the next. We have seen how she was stirred by the call of God and how this drove her, like Christ himself, out into the relative wilderness of a break with her past. From this grew a new beginning, so the energy ran inward again toward the centre as she and [her sister] Agnes found their feet at San Damiano. Then a community began to gather and Clare's influence spread further afield. Yet she herself remained faithful to the inner source of her energy which then led her on to other challenges, such as the extraordinary expansion of her way of life, or the insights about Islam brought to her from the East by Francis. So the inner deepening and the outer extension developed together. As her roots sank deeper, so her branches spread wider.

Frances Teresa OSC

21

An old man said, 'There are monks who do many good works, and the evil one sends them scruples about quite little things, to cause them to lose the fruit of the good they have done. When I happened to be living in Oxyrhynchus near a priest who gave alms to many, a widow came to ask him for some wheat. He said to her, "Bring a sack and I will measure some out for you." She brought it, and measuring the sack with his hand, he said, "It is a big sack." Now this filled the widow with shame. I said to him, "Abba, have you sold the wheat?" He said, "No, I gave it her in charity." I said to him, "If you gave it all to her in alms, why did you cavil at the amount and fill her with shame?"'

A Desert Father

22

'And then there were the two brothers who lived on the far side of the desert at Thebais, where the blessed Antony had been. Traveling across the vast emptiness of that uninhabited region they were moved by a lapse of discernment to resolve that the only food they would take would be whatever the Lord himself offered them. They were staggering through the desert, weak from hunger, when they were spotted from a distance by the Mazices. This is a people more savage and cruel than almost any other tribe. Some shed blood for the sake of loot but these are stirred by sheer ferocity. And yet in spite of their innate barbarism they rushed with bread to the two men.

'One of the [two], moved by discernment, accepted with joy and blessing the food offered him, as if it were the Lord himself who was giving it. In his view the food had been made available by God himself. It had to be God's work that those who always rejoiced in the shedding of blood were now giving of what they had to weak and wasted men.

'The other man refused the food. It had been offered by man. And he died of hunger.

'Both had started out with a wrong decision. One, however, with the help of discernment changed his mind about something which he had rashly and imprudently decided. The other man stuck to his foolish presumptuousness. Knowing nothing about discernment he drew down upon himself the death which the

Lord had wished to avert. He would not believe that at God's instigation wild barbarians had so forgotten their innate savagery as to come with bread instead of with the sword.'

John Cassian (Abba Moses speaking)

23

The monk may think he has come [to the monastery] to gain something for himself: peace, security, quiet, a life of prayer, or study, or teaching; but if his vocation is genuine, he finds that he has come not to take but to give – or, more accurately, to be shaped as an instrument of God's action. St Benedict calls on his monks to expend their talents in God's service; so that 'we may serve him', to quote the Prologue to the Rule, 'with the gifts which he has given us'.

Aelred Graham OSB

24

If the space between the ideologies of right and left is becoming ever smaller, the number of poor and oppressed who occupy this space, that is to say, the victims of these two extremist attitudes, is becoming ever greater. The mission of monastics to be men and women of communion calls them today to communion with the enormous masses of expatriates, of refugees, of unemployed. Benedictine hospitality is needed more than ever. Benedict had foreseen this hospitality for the poor, the pilgrims and the homeless.

Armand Veilleux OCSO

25

You owe it to yourself. This is the proverb of the one who clutches the good things – money, time, pleasures – tightly to oneself, surrendering nothing. The reward system is built in and functions smoothly. The consumer mentality, on this principle, plays into the hand of the myriad industries eager to cater to every desire and turn a profit. The ego is at the center of the world, firmly ensconced, like a spider jealously guarding its web and drawing everything in.

What this mentality reveals is greed, that most profound and insatiable desire of the human heart. But hidden deep within the damning dictum is the echo of Augustine's cry: 'Our hearts are made for you, O Lord, and they are restless until they rest in you.' Nothing so reveals the true destiny of the human spirit as this insatiable quest for more and more. This most powerful of all human instincts leads, if we will but lift our eyes, toward the Infinite Love which we do, indeed, 'owe' to ourselves.

Hilary Ottensmeyer OSB

26

Once there was a monk
who was
lazy,
angry,
lustful,
complained about the food,
who argued with everyone,
hollered,
even was a little paranoid;
but the words of the Rule came clear:
'Seek forgiveness before sunset.'

The monk died of heart failure
at an early age,
result of daily rushing to beat
the sun,
(though some called it
the pace of modern life.)
Anyway,
that monk
is revered
a saint.

Suzanne Zuercher OSB

27

Why is it so difficult to acknowledge a gift as a gift? Here is the
reason. When I admit that something is a gift, I admit my dependence on the giver. This may not sound that difficult, but there is
something within us that bristles at the idea of dependence. We
want to get along by ourselves. Yet a gift is something we simply
cannot give to ourselves – not as a gift, at any rate. I can buy the
same thing or even something better. But it will not be a gift if I
procure it for myself. I can go out and treat myself to a magnifi-
cent treat. I can even be grateful later for the good time I had. But
can I be grateful to myself for having treated myself so well? That
would be neck-breaking mental acrobatics. Gratefulness always
goes beyond myself. For what makes something a gift is precisely
that it is given. And the receiver depends on the giver.

This dependence is always there when a gift is given and
received ... Gift giving is a celebration of the bond that unites
giver and receiver. That bond is gratefulness.

David Steindl-Rast OSB

28

Real joy is very deep-rooted and we have to dig down deeply within ourselves to bring something of it to the surface. This must be the meaning of the expression we may use spontaneously when we speak of being very happy: 'I am deeply happy.' For that reason all great happiness is 'speechless'. It cannot be voiced. It is inexpressible. It seldom comes to the surface and we can never show it off. We are 'inhabited' by our joy, somewhere close to the roots of our being.

Joy is the seed-bed in which all life strikes root in order to be able to manage its own existence. Without joy we cannot live or, rather, we cannot survive. Joy wells up, especially at extraordinary moments in which we may experience our own reality or the beauty of life. Think of the joy that art can furnish, 'a thing of beauty is a joy for ever'. In the enjoyment of art genuine delight arises in us precisely because through it we can discover and, as it were, touch the very essence of people and things. It is not something we observe in the usual way through the senses, nor something that can be verbalized – this deep reality in others and in ourselves. Thus joy is always a sign that we have been granted a deeper sense of communion with 'being' or 'existence' itself.

André Louf OCSO

29

It is trust in the limits of the self that makes us open and it is trust in the gifts of others that makes us secure. We come to realize that we don't have to do everything, that we can't do everything, that what I can't do is someone else's gift and responsibility. I am a small piece of the cosmic clock, a necessary piece but not the only piece. My limitations make space for the gifts of other people. Without the grace of our limitations we would be isolated, dry, and insufferable creatures indeed. It is our limitations and the trust, the dependence on others, that springs from them that save us from all the tiny little deaths that struggle brings.

Joan Chittister OSB

30

When I was young, of course I rightly wanted to do great things for God. As my vocation was to be a contemplative nun, I suppose I meant I wanted to be able to pray like St Clare. Well, without that desire I should have got nowhere. I most certainly wanted to help others by my prayer – and I took it for granted that I should know I was doing so. Now I am old, I know that it is his action, not mine. I can only pray the prayer God gives me to pray – and if he does not give me any prayers, that does not really matter – he can use even that. I now view 'waste of time' differently. It is not the intrinsic value of how I am occupied that is important. It is the attitude with which I am living. Brooding on what happened yesterday or worrying about how I am going to be able to cope tomorrow, these are the wasted time. It is today I am in peace to love and serve the Lord.

Elsie Felicity OSC

December

Endings and beginnings

Let them prefer nothing whatever to Christ, and may he bring us all
alike to everlasting life.

Rule of Benedict, Chapter 72

I

The quest for God, the never to be completely satisfied longing for God, is worth one's life. Do not be afraid to forfeit whatever owns you, whatever idols capture your heart. This is your joy. A single-minded focus on Christ will help you to survive and give you courage and insight even in darkness. Those choose and possess the treasure who can hold on to God as their source and affirmation not only in joy but even when their great desire seems disappointed by life.

Constance Fitzgerald OCD

2

The soul that journeys to God, but does not shake off its cares and quiet its appetites, is like one who drags a cart uphill.

John of the Cross

3

A young monk once went to see his superior: 'Father,' he said, 'I must leave the monastery because I clearly do not have a vocation to be a monk.' When the older monk asked why, the younger monk replied: 'In spite of daily resolutions to be good-tempered, chaste and sober, I keep on sinning. So I feel I am not suited to the monastic life.' The older monk looked at him with love and said: 'Brother, the monastic life is this: I rise up and I fall down, I rise up and I fall down, I rise up and I fall down.' The young monk stayed and persevered.

Christopher Jamison OSB

4

The sacrifices involved in monastic life are frequently chronicled, but we ought not to forget the hundredfold. There is a certain beauty that is a consequence of spending most of one's life in a single pursuit, attached to one place, and living with the same people. We are at liberty to be ourselves, no longer hiding behind facades or masks. Yet this self is more than the fleeting persona of this present moment; it is a self that stretches expansively over many years and decades, full of seeming contradictions and subject to so many vicissitudes. We are surrounded by so many memories of times past, of people now in heaven, of projects completed or left undone, of trees planted, of griefs and joys. As we pass through the monastery and listen to the echoes embedded in its walls, the refrain we hear is, 'This is your life.' Because of these voices we are compelled to live at a high level of truthfulness, since we cannot escape from what we have been and still are. A strong sense of continuity develops, and a deeper feeling of acceptance. This is where I belong. This is my home. Here I live; here I will die.

Michael Casey OCSO

5

How difficult it is to live in the creative tension of hope, the tension between not-yet and already! When we allow that tension to snap, our quest peters out in aimless wandering or gets stuck in a compulsive settling down. We see this all around us, even among religious folk. There are those who want everything already.

They cannot be bothered with a not-yet. Getting there is all that matters to them. They want things settled once and for all, and the sooner the better. Searching is a nuisance for them. Their counterparts, on the other hand, are so enamored with searching that finding becomes a threat. Finding would put an end to the search. It would spoil the game. The thrill they find in the quest lies exclusively in the not-yet.

David Steindl-Rast OSB

6

If we would become wise we must learn that we have here no abiding city (Hebrews 13:14).

To have life in focus we must have death in our field of vision. Within this vision we see life as preparation for death and death as preparation for life.

If we are to meet our own death with hope it must be a hope built not on theory or on belief alone but on experience. We must know from experience that death is an event in life, an essential part of any life which is lived as a perpetually expanding and self-transcending mystery.

Only the experience of the continuous death of the ego can lead us into this hope, into an ever-deepening contact with the power of life itself.

Only our death to self-centredness can really persuade us of death as the connecting link in the chain of perpetual expansion, and as the way to fullness of life.

John Main OSB

7

We gain nothing by our decision to renounce earthly things if we do not abide by it, but continue to be attracted by such things and allow ourselves to keep thinking about them. By constantly looking back ... towards what we have renounced we make clear our attachment to it ...

What does the law mean when it commands anyone entering the temple not to return, after finishing his prayers, by the door through which he entered, but go straight out through the opposite door without changing direction? It means that we should keep to the path that leads straight to holiness, not allowing any doubts to make us turn back. By habitually thinking about what we have left behind, we undermine our determination to advance and we are pulled in the opposite direction, returning to our old sins. It is a terrible thing when the force of habit holds us fast, not allowing us to rise to the state of virtue which we possessed initially. For habit leads to a set disposition, and this in turn becomes what may be called 'second nature'; and it is hard to shift and alter nature. For though it may yield a little to pressure, it quickly reasserts itself. It may be shaken and forced to give way, but it is not permanently changed, unless through prolonged effort we retrace our steps.

Neilos the Ascetic

8

When people ask me why I became a monk, I feel very like the engaged couple who are asked why they have fallen in love. We don't really know. What they *can* say, and I equally, is that certain things have happened to us in our lives which made us come to a decision. But very often when I am asked why I became a monk, what I am really being asked is: Why did I run away? Why am I trying to escape from real life? My only answer to this is that I don't think it is true. Nor do I feel that by becoming a monk I have made myself a prisoner, locked away from the world. Although I am only too aware that I don't deserve it, my time as a monk and later as a monk-priest has been a wonderful experience. There have been times ... when I have been tempted to pack up and leave and I expect there will be such times again in the future. But this is something which, as I have begun to understand, happens to most people: the grass can so often look greener on the other side. In reality my life in the monastery has been very exciting and fulfilled. I have learned a great deal from others, both inside and outside the monastery.

Leonard Vickers OSB

9

For me the chief form of suffering has been mental, not physical, as I have been blessed (so far) with good health. It is rather inner fear, feelings of guilt and failure, worry about the future for myself and others which have been most painful. What is most extraordinary is that gradually I have come to see that the most unwanted and painful inner suffering is actually a means of being drawn closer to God. The face of God as of one who loves and is lovable above all things is actually revealed through such experiences. The whole thing is most strange and paradoxical: what human lover would treat his beloved in this way? For me it is the most practical and genuine witness to the truth of the Christian mystery that personal suffering does bring greater peace of mind, a sense of joy and a greater capacity to love and be loved. At the time one can rage and try to escape, feel that one is going further and further away from God and that hope is really lost, and yet later one knows that only thus could one be given a deeper understanding and experience of the mystery of God. Through cross to resurrection is indeed the grammar of the language of the true God.

David Morland OSB

10

I feel more and more the paradox of my vocation, such as it is. This is my place and yet I have never felt so strongly that I have 'no place' as I have felt here since becoming fully reconciled to this as 'my place.' My place is in reality no place, and I hesitate to act as if I were anything but a stranger anywhere, but especially here. I am an alien and a transient and this is the last happiness that is possible to me: but a very real one. More real than all the others I thought I knew before it. Everything is alien to me and I am alien to everything, even contemplation, even writing. I have no longer a profession, although there is no getting away from the fact that in the end I have come out as a 'writer,' if categories count for anything.

Thomas Merton

11

My monastery is on a hill ...

A place and the lives that unfold in a place inevitably interpenetrate, and there is a reciprocal exchange between them such that each composes the other and accompanies the other. Affection grows. Monks love their place, and the place loves its monks. As the years of my searching for God in this place pass, I love the place more and more because progressively its features and details are gathered into my story. This love stirs in me with every ascent or descent of the hill. If I go down the hill, I am on my way elsewhere and I feel the difference as I descend. If my absence is to be a long one, the emotion of leaving what I love is more sharply borne. On returning from afar, however far, it is in the start of the ascent that I know I am returned home. In the short time it takes to mount upward to the top, all the complicated emotions of what it means to live in this place flash through me and resolve themselves in the climb.

Jeremy Driscoll OSB

12

There may come a day when my glory will sing to him, and when my conscience will not feel compunction, where all sighs and fears will have ceased; but in the meantime, in silence and hope will be my strength. I want to live and die in striving and hoping for eternal life more than for the possession of all creatures and all their goods; for these will come to an end. Don't abandon me, Lord, because I hope that in you my hope will not be confounded; may I always serve you; and do with me whatever you will.

Teresa of Avila

13

Our disobedience is that we want to be in control – the one thing for which we are not fitted, so we worry about the future ... We long to know how God is going to run things, especially us, and we are always seduced by the chance of knowledge about what will hit us next, what will be good and what evil. That is like a bite taken from the fruit of the tree of knowledge. Yet chewing that bite is so against our true nature that it instantly becomes a poisonous fruit for us, destroying our freedom and bringing disaster ... Our dilemma is that, while goodness is simple, badness is easy and we want both. No wonder our spiritual technology is so primitive when we spend our lives rediscovering the wheel; yet any acorn knows how to roll downhill. Most of us could learn wisdom from that acorn.

Frances Teresa OSC

14

The struggle with powerlessness is the struggle for effectiveness, yes, but more than that it is the struggle for simplicity of heart. However much we have cultivated an image of the imperious, the aura of invincibility, the patina of the supremely secure, we are helpless to help ourselves. Life as we have known it ends. We are confronted with the puniness of our existence. We come face to face with our mortality, our vulnerability, our limitations. Now we must become who we really are, not who we have presented ourselves to be. Now simplicity – our basic, core self – takes over.

Joan Chittister OSB

15

Abba Lot went to see Abba Joseph and said: Abba, as much as I am able I practice a small rule, a little fasting, some prayer and meditation, and remain quiet, and as much as possible I keep my thoughts clean. What else should I do? Then the old man stood up and stretched out his hands toward heaven, and his fingers became like ten torches of flame. And he said: If you wish, you can become all flame.

Abba Joseph

16

The story is told of St Francis that one day he and his brothers came to a crossroads. Francis shut his eyes while the others spun round and round, and when he shouted 'Stop!' they went off, in whatever direction they were facing, to convert the world. This story is a neat image of the experience of conversion, for it, too, means coming to a crossroads where we go into an apparently random spin which, when it eventually slows to a halt, leaves us facing who knows where, except that the direction will radically affect the rest of our lives. Often our co-operation with grace will, at first, mean nothing more than surrender to spinning as an image of our surrender to God so that, for us as for the brothers, the direction we are to take can be made clear.

Frances Teresa OSC

17

testament

my body is for the earth
but please
no preservative
between it and me
my heart is for life
but please
no affectation
between it and me
my hands for work
will be folded
quite simply
as for my face
let it be bare
so as not to hinder a kiss
and my gaze
let it SEE
P.S.
thanks

Christophe Lebreton OSCO

18

Christian de Chergé wrote this Testament about two years before he and six of his fellow monks were kidnapped and murdered in Algeria during a time of intense unrest in that country.

Facing a GOODBYE ...
If it should happen one day – and it could be today –
that I become a victim of the terrorism which now seems ready
    to engulf all the foreigners living in Algeria,
I would like my community, my Church and my family
to remember that my life was GIVEN to God and to this
    country.
I ask them to accept the fact that the One master of all life
was not a stranger to this brutal departure.
I would ask them to pray for me:
for how could I be found worthy of such an offering?
I ask them to associate this death with so many other violent
    ones
which are forgotten through indifference or anonymity.
My life has no more value than any other.
Nor any less value.
...
And you also, my last-minute friend, who will not have known
    what you were doing:
Yes, I want this THANK YOU and this GOODBYE to be a
    'GOD-BLESS' for you too,
because in God's face I see yours.
May we meet again as happy thieves in Paradise, if it please
    God, the Father of us both.
AMEN! INCHALLAH!

Christian de Chergé OCSO

19

BUT ONE THING WILL NOT CHANGE. The essential nature of religious life as a walk into the arms of God, without security, without certainty of success, without the kind of status that makes the rest of the world go round, without fear of death in a life that swears that it lives in the light of the Resurrection.

The present decline in numbers of religious breaks open for each of us old questions in new ways. We must ask ourselves again, 'Why did I come to religious life?' And more to the point, 'Why do I stay?' It is time for purification of spirit. Theology itself has perhaps corrupted our motives, culture has warped our ends, society has trivialized our existence, time has cut us down in mid-flight. But historically, it is just as possible that we are simply being trimmed for travel, prepared for new life, brought to exodus again for new times, new needs, in a new way. Our own as well as the needs of the world in which we live.

Joan Chittister OSB

20

Perhaps the most perplexing moment of the Jesus stories is that cry of desperation from the cross, 'My God, my God, why have you forsaken me?' (Mark 15.34). His body torn apart by human cruelty, Jesus knows he is about to die. He is frightened to the core of his being. Here is a human being humiliated and degraded – hardly a just end for one who was so compassionate to all he met. And, as his sensitivity is so acute, the more sharply does he feel the suffering. He can no longer stand it and cries out in words that jumble a despair (an answerless void) with prayer (that basic affirming connection with God).

... Towards prayer suffering remains ambivalent. Suffering can at times mute our positive relation with God and can even blot out our religious desires. That possibility must never be forgotten.

It was admirably remembered by John Henry Newman writing his mystical poem on the experience of dying:

> 'Tis this new feeling, never felt before ...
> That I am going, that I am no more.
> 'Tis this strange innermost abandonment ...
> This emptying out of each constituent
> And natural force, by which I come to be.

Matthias Neuman OSB

21

The question is not 'Do institutions die?' but 'How do they? And how do we respond to their dying?' Are we aware or do we prefer the apparent safety of denial? When denial is no longer possible, what do we do then? Rage against the inevitable? Give up? Bargain for more time? Or do we face institutional death with courage, living the present to the full, admitting that life's precariousness is part of its preciousness? The choice of response is ours, not only as individuals, but as communities. Instant communication provides information; it does not ensure adequate response nor delay death's inevitability. Institutions must die, but how they die is a matter for decision. Ours!

Marie Beha OSC

22

The ammas [Desert Mothers] taught me that the way out of the frenzied pace of our culture involves both external and internal journeys. I simplified possessions and needs. I am committed to owning less, not accumulating more. I let go of all commitments and activities that did not support or fit in with my life goals. Friendships are fewer but deeper and richer. Do we give ourselves permission to say 'No' – to self and to others? Do we live intentionally, making choices by our values and goals? Do we give away everything we haven't used in the last six months?

I began literally to slow down. I am learning to be more mindful of what I am doing while I am doing it. I am not so scattered, with my mind drifting in so many directions. I am deepening the awareness of God's presence throughout my day. I stop to breathe, take note of where I am and what I am doing, and notice the Spirit in the midst of my do-ing.

Laura Swan OSB

23

We are made in the very image of God, so we are mystery. We are question, infinite question. We can avoid living in the question only by avoiding our true self, devoting ourselves to building up a false self made up of what I do, what I have, what others think of me. We want to have 'the answer' – the answer that will answer all, so that we can have everything under control, so that we can sense the power.

God is the answer. And God is mystery, God is the question.

Basil Pennington OCSO

24

So then, beloved brothers and sisters, let us be careful that no unseemliness degrades us – seeing that, in the eternal foresight, we are both citizens of God and equals of his angels. Let us lay claim to our honor by the way we live. Let no immorality stain us, no shameful thought accuse us, no evil intent plague our minds, none of the rust of envy eat into us, no conceit puff us up, no ambition weaken us with earthly beckonings, no anger set us on fire. For human beings are called gods. Be answerable for yourself, then, against the vices for the honor of God since, for your sake, God became man.

Gregory the Great

25

Oh God, we are one with You. You have made us one with You. You have taught us that if we are open to one another, You dwell in us. Help us to preserve this openness and to fight for it with all our hearts. Help us to realize that there can be no understanding where there is mutual rejection. Oh God, in accepting one another wholeheartedly, fully, completely, we accept You, and we thank You, and we adore You, and we love You with our whole being, because our being is in Your being, our spirit is rooted in Your spirit. Fill us then with love, and let us be bound together with love ... united in this one spirit which makes You present in the world, and which makes You witness to the ultimate reality that is love. Love has overcome. Love is victorious. Amen.

Thomas Merton

26

They used to tell of an old man who was dying at Scetis. His brethren were standing round his bed putting the habit on him and weeping, but he opened his eyes and laughed; then he laughed a second and third time. The brothers asked him, 'Abba, tell us how it is that while we are weeping you laugh.' He said to them, 'I laughed because you all fear death; I laughed a second time because you are not ready; and I laughed a third time because I am leaving labour for rest.' And immediately the old man fell asleep.

A Desert Father

27

It is always an illusion to think that one has been converted once and for all. The truth is we are always merely sinners, forgiven sinners, that is, sinners-in-a-state-of-forgiveness, sinners-in-the-process-of-conversion. On earth there can be no other holiness, because grace does not relate to us in any other way. To repent is ever and again to take our place in this inner reversal: the turning of our human finiteness – Paul calls it 'flesh' – toward the grace of God. It is a turning from the law of the letter to the law of the Spirit and of freedom, from wrath to grace. This reversal is never finished, because the truth is that it has always only just started. Anthony the Great, the well-known patriarch and father of all monks, said it pithily: 'Every morning again I say to myself, today I start.' And Abba Poemen, after Anthony the second most famous of the ancient fathers, when on his death-bed people congratulated him because after a blessed and virtuous life he was permitted to go out to meet God in full confidence, replied: 'I am still a beginner; I had barely started with my conversion.' And as he said this, he wept.

André Louf OCSO

28

Charles Williams describes on the first page [of *All Hallows Eve*] the soul of his dead heroine on one of the bridges of London where she died. She sees nothing but herself, the point at which her feet touch the ground and the aeroplane which crashed and killed her. She sees nothing because her heart is attached to nothing ... She has no key to the world around her because she has never loved anything and is a stranger here. Suddenly her husband, now her widower, walks over the bridge. They see each other, he because he loves her and he bears her in his heart, weeps for her and seeks her in the invisible world, she because he is the only person she has ever loved in her poor selfish way. He is the only person she can see. She sees him. He goes on. But her heart has stirred and through her husband she remembers her world, husband, their home and friends. And gradually, through this love she begins to discover the world she has lived in without knowing it and at the same time the new vast world she has just entered ... For we only see what we love. We think we see what we hate, but really in our hatred we see only deformed images, caricatures. And indifference and lukewarmness are blind.

Anthony Bloom

29

I finally reached Kedarnath [a Hindu holy place] in the afternoon, quite exhausted and surrounded by a thick mist which covered up and hid everything and penetrated everything with its icy humidity. Nothing could be seen of the high peaks of twenty to twenty-five thousand feet which, I was told, towered directly above. I could scarcely make out the outline of the temple which stands up at the far end of the village at the exact spot where the numerous trickles of water from the lip of the glacier untie to form a stream, the Mandakini. I contented myself with wandering through the hamlet looking for food and shelter for the night. When I was given a room I shut myself in, wrapped myself in my blankets and tried to sleep.

Towards midnight I suddenly woke up. I then had the idea of opening the door a few inches and risking a quick look into the icy night. What a marvellous sight! Not a trace of the mist ...

Dazzling beauty outside and a dazed feeling within. Is not everything a sign? A sign of the one unique Mystery; the groping towards the mysterious place of this unfathomable origin of oneself, symbolized both by the circle of snowy mountains and by the summit of the path; the depth from where everything issues forth and expands and the point of consummation towards which all things tend, where the road comes to an end and where all is fulfilled.

Abhishiktananda (Henri le Saux OSB)

30

The heart, dear friends, that covets the sight of God as in a mirror must keep itself free from worldly cares, from harmful, unnecessary and even necessary ones. It must keep itself ever alert through reading, meditation and prayer. Blessed are the pure of heart; they shall see God. May he grant that we do so. Amen.

Isaac of Stella

31

In our monasteries, we have been content to find our way to a kind of peace, a simple undisturbed thoughtful life. And this is certainly good, but is it good enough?

I, for one, realize that now I need more. Not simply to be quiet, somewhat productive, to pray, to read, to cultivate leisure – *otium sanctum* [holy leisure]! There is a need of effort, deepening, change and transformation. Not that I must undertake a special project of self-transformation or that I must 'work on myself.' In that regard, it would be better to forget it. Just to go for walks, live in peace, let change come quietly and invisibly on the inside.

But I do have a past to break with, an accumulation of inertia, waste, wrong, foolishness, rot, junk, a great need of clarification of mindfulness, or rather of no mind – a return to genuine practice, right effort, need to push on to the great doubt. Need for the Spirit.

Hang on to the clear light!

Thomas Merton

List of sources

The quotations from the Rule of Benedict are the compilers', with a heavy debt to Justin McCann OSB, *The Rule of Saint Benedict in Latin and English* (London: Burns and Oates, 1952); and to Joan D. Chittister, *The Rule of Benedict: Insights for the Ages* (Slough: St Pauls, 1992).

The quotations from the Long Rules of Basil the Great are based on *Saint Basil: The Long Rules*, trans. M. Monica Wagner CSC, in the series Selections from the Fathers of the Church in Pamphlet Form (Boston MA: Daughters of St Paul, 1952).

All the quotations from *The Sayings of the Desert Fathers: The Alphabetical Collection*, trans. Benedicta Ward SLG (Oxford: A. R. Mowbray/Kalamazoo MI: Cistercian Publications, 1975, 1984) are used by kind permission of Continuum International Publishing Group.

The compilers regret that they have been unable to find a way of contacting the translator, publisher or their representative, in the case of the verse translation of Gregory of Narek on September 16.

January

1 Aquinata Böckmann OSB, *Perspectives on the Rule of St Benedict: Expanding Our Hearts in Christ* (Collegeville MN: The Liturgical Press, 2005, German original 1986), pp. 15 and 16.

2 Basil Pennington OCSO, *Who Do You Say That I Am? Meditations on Jesus' Questions in the Gospels* (Hyde Park NY: New City Press, 1999), p. 7.

3 Laura Swan OSB, *Engaging Benedict: What the Rule Can Teach Us Today* (Notre Dame IN: Ave Maria Press, 2005), p. 7.

4 Basil the Great, from Letter 2 (Benedictine arrangement), trans. compilers.

5 *Desert Wisdom: Sayings from the Desert Fathers*, trans. Yushi Nomura (New York: Doubleday & Company, Inc., 1982), p. 1.

6 Jean Leclercq OSB, 'Tradition: A Door to the Present', *Monastic Studies* 4 (Pine City NY: Mount Saviour Monastery, 1966), p. 13f.

7 Benedict Auer OSB, *Soulpoeting: Healing through Poetry* (London: St Pauls, 2000), p. 27. Used by permission of St Pauls (formerly St Paul Publications), UK.

8 André Louf OCSO, *Tuning in to Grace: The Quest for God*, trans. John Vriend (London: Darton, Longman & Todd, 1992), p. 137.

9 Joan Chittister OSB, *The Rule of Benedict: Insights for the Ages* (Slough: St Paul Publications, 1992), p. 33.

10 Thomas Keating OCSO, *The Human Condition: Contemplation and Transformation* (New York and Mahwah NJ: Paulist Press, 1999), p. 17.

11 Basil Hume OSB, *To Be a Pilgrim: A Spiritual Notebook* (Slough: St Paul Publications, 1984), p. 38.

12 John Main OSB, *John Main: Arranged for Daily Reading*, comp. Clare Hallward (London: Darton, Longman & Todd, 1987; Springfield IL: Templegate Publishers, 1988), p. 67.

13 The 'Brief Rule' of St Romuald, from Bruno-Boniface of Querfurt, *The Life of the Five Brothers*, trans. Thomas Matus in *The Mystery of Romuald and the Five Brothers* (Big Sur: Hermitage Books, 1994), p. 95.

14 A Carthusian, *Where Silence is Praise* (London: Darton, Longman & Todd, 1997), p. 9.

15 Anthony Bloom, *Living Prayer* (London: Darton, Longman & Todd, 1966), p. 65.

16 Thomas Keating OCSO, *Open Mind, Open Heart: The Contemplative Dimension of the Gospel* (Rockport MA and Shaftesbury: Element Books, 1991), pp. 33–4.

17 Jean Chively OSC, 'Enclosure: Sacramental Sign', *Review for Religious* 54/3 (May/June 1995), p. 461.

18 John Main OSB, *Letters from the Heart: Christian Monasticism and the Renewal of Community* (New York: Crossroad, 1988), p. 89.

19 Marie Beha OSC, 'Becoming Contemplative: Here or There', *Review for Religious* 51/5 (September/October 1992), pp. 745–6.

20 Laura Swan OSB, *Engaging Benedict: What the Rule Can Teach Us Today* (Notre Dame IN: Ave Maria Press, 2005), pp. 74–5.

21 André Louf OCSO, *The Cistercian Alternative*, trans. Nivard Kinsella o.cist. (Gill & Macmillan, 1983), p. 22.

22 Timothy Wright OSB in Kit Dollard, Anthony Marett-Crosby OSB, Abbot Timothy Wright OSB, *The Rule of St Benedict and Business Management: A Conversation* (London and New York: Continuum, 2002), p. 198.

23 Timothy Wright OSB in Kit Dollard, Anthony Marett-Crosby OSB, Abbot Timothy Wright OSB, *The Rule of St Benedict and Business Management: A Conversation* (London and New York: Continuum, 2002), p. 201.

24 Kurt Stasiak OSB, 'What Child Is This God?', *Assembly* 21/4 (November 1995), p. 688.

25 Albert Holtz OSB, *Street Wisdom: Connecting with God in Everyday Life* (Mystic CT: Twenty-Third Publications, 2003), p. 1.

26 William McNamara OCD, *The Human Adventure: The Art of Contemplative Living* (Warwick NY: Amity House, 1974), pp. 160–1.

27 Marie Beha osc, 'Culture and Contemplative Community', *Review for Religious* 52/4 (July/August 1993), p. 591.

28 John Climacus, *The Ladder of Divine Ascent*, trans. Colm Luibhead and Norman Russell (Mahwah NJ: Paulist Press/London: SPCK, 1982), Step 26, p. 237 (slightly adapted).

29 Gregory the Great, from homily 27 on the Gospel (John 15.12–16), trans. Aelred Squire, in *Fathers Talking: An Anthology* (Kalamazoo MI: Cistercian Publications, 1986), pp. 21–2.

30 Joan Chittister osb, 'The Fall of the Temple – A Call to Formation', *Religious Life Review* Vol. 43 (January/February 2004), p. 59.

31 Anselm of Canterbury, *Proslogion*, ch. 26, trans. M. J. Charlesworth in *St Anselm's Proslogion* (Oxford: Clarendon Press, 1965), p. 153.

February

1 Laura Swan osb, from *The Forgotten Desert Mothers: Sayings, Lives and Stories of Early Christian Women* (New York/Mahwah NJ: Paulist Press, 2001), p. 152.

2 Abhishiktananda (Henri le Saux osb), *Guru and Disciple*, trans. Heather Sandeman (London: SPCK, 1974), pp. 6–7.

3 Kallistos Ware, from 'The Spiritual Father in Orthodox Christianity', *Cross Currents* (Summer/Fall 1974), pp. 296–313; see also http://www.orthodoxinfo.com/praxis/spiritualfather.

4 Michael Casey ocso, *Strangers to the City: Reflections on the Beliefs and Values of the Rule of Saint Benedict* (Brewster MA: Paraclete Press, 2005), p. 102.

5 Macarius the Great, from *The Sayings of the Desert Fathers: The Alphabetical Collection*, trans. Benedicta Ward slg (Kalamazoo MI: Cistercian Publications/ Oxford: A. R. Mowbray, 1975, revised edn 1984), p. 131.

6 Archimandrite Sophrony (Sakharov), *We Shall See Him as He Is*, trans. Rosemary Edmonds (Tolleshunt Knights, Essex: The Patriarchal Stavropegic Monastery of St John the Baptist, 1987), p. 64.

7 Frances Teresa osc, *This Living Mirror: Reflections on Clare of Assisi* (London: Darton, Longman & Todd, 1995), p. 25.

8 Ruth Burrows, *To Believe in Jesus* (London: Sheed and Ward, 1978), pp. 95–6.

9 Joan D. Chittister osb, *Twelve Steps to Inner Freedom: Humility Revisited* (Erie PA: Benetvision, 2003), p. 33.

10 *The Sayings of the Desert Fathers: The Alphabetical Collection*, trans. Benedicta Ward slg (Kalamazoo MI: Cistercian Publications/Oxford: A. R. Mowbray, 1975, revised edn 1984), p. 190.

11 Michael Casey ocso, *Sacred Writing: The Ancient Art of Lectio Divina* (Liguori MO: Liguori/Triumph, 1995), p. 74.

12 *The Desert Fathers: Sayings of the Early Christian Monks*, trans. Benedicta Ward slg (London: Penguin Books, 2003), p. 5.

13   James McCaffrey OCD, 'Carmelite Forum: Sharing a Heritage', *Religious Life Review* Vol. 40 (September/October 2001), p. 271.

14   *The Sayings of the Desert Fathers: The Alphabetical Collection*, trans. Benedicta Ward SLG (Kalamazoo MI: Cistercian Publications/Oxford: A. R. Mowbray, 1975, revised edn 1984), pp. 83–4.

15   Aquinata Böckmann OSB, *Perspectives on the Rule of St Benedict: Expanding Our Heart in Christ* (Collegeville, MN: The Liturgical Press, 2005; German original 1986), p. 18.

16   Aelred, *Spiritual Friendship* 2:11, trans. Mary Eugenia Laker SSND (Washington DC: Cistercian Publications, 1977), pp. 72.

17   Columba Stewart OSB, *Prayer and Community: The Benedictine Tradition* (London: Darton, Longman & Todd, 1998), p. 87.

18   *The Sayings of the Desert Fathers: The Alphabetical Collection*, trans. Benedicta Ward SLG (Kalamazoo MI: Cistercian Publications/Oxford: A. R. Mowbray, 1975, revised edn 1984), pp. 138–9.

19   John Main OSB, *John Main: Arranged for Daily Reading*, comp. Clare Hallward (London: Darton, Longman & Todd, 1987/Springfield IL: Templegate Publishers, 1988), pp. 14–15.

20   Antony the Great (attributed), in 'On the Character of Men and on the Virtuous Life', *The Philokalia*, trans. G. E. H. Palmer, Philip Sherrard and Kallistos Ware (London: Faber & Faber 1983 [1979]), pp. 330-1.

21   Anthony Bloom, 'My Monastic Life', *Cistercian Studies* 8 (1973/3), pp. 194–5.

22   Joan D. Chittister OSB, *Twelve Steps to Inner Freedom: Humility Revisited* (Erie PA: Benetvision, 2003), p. 30.

23   Seraphim of Sarov, quoted in Irina Gorainov, *The Message of Saint Seraphim* (Oxford: SLG Press, 1973), p. 14.

24   *The Sayings of the Desert Fathers: The Alphabetical Collection*, trans. Benedicta Ward SLG (Kalamazoo MI: Cistercian Publications/Oxford: A. R. Mowbray, 1975, revised edn 1984), p. 174.

25   Albert Holtz OSB, *Street Wisdom: Connecting with God in Everyday Life* (Mystic CT: Twenty-Third Publications, 2003), p. 35.

26   Basil Pennington OCSO, *Who Do You Say That I Am? Meditations on Jesus' Questions in the Gospels* (Hyde Park NY: New City Press, 1999), pp. 8–9.

27   Evagrius Ponticus, nos. 32 and 33 of the *Chapters on Prayer* in *Evagrius Ponticus – The Praktikos and Chapters on Prayer*, trans. John Eudes Bamberger OCSO (Spencer MA: Cistercian Publications, 1970), p. 60.

28   *The Sayings of the Desert Fathers: the Alphabetical Collection*, trans. Benedicta Ward SLG (Kalamazoo MI: Cistercian Publications/London: A. R. Mowbray, 1975, revised edn 1984), p. 2.

29   Joan D. Chittister OSB, *Heart of Flesh: A Feminist Spirituality for Women and Men* (Grand Rapids MI, and Cambridge, UK: Eerdmans; Saint Paul University, Ottawa: Novalis, 1998), p. 98.

March

1 *The Desert Fathers: Sayings of the Early Christian Monks*, trans. Benedicta Ward SLG (London: Penguin Books, 2003), p. 71.

2 Joan D. Chittister OSB, *Twelve Steps to Inner Freedom: Humility Revisited* (Erie PA: Benetvision, 2003), p. 17.

3 *Desert Wisdom: Saying from the Desert Fathers*, trans. Yushi Nomura (Garden City NY: Doubleday & Co., 1982), p. 95.

4 Christine Vladimiroff OSB, 'Reflections on the Monastic Life: Community' at http://www.eriebenedictines.org/Pages/INSPIRATION/backprioress/Community.html (accessed 10/04/2006).

5 Aelred of Rievaulx, *Spiritual Friendship* (Washington DC: Cistercian Publications, 1977), pp. 94–5.

6 André Louf OCSO, *The Cistercian Alternative*, trans. Nivard Kinsella O cist (London: Gill & Macmillan, 1983), p. 126.

7 Timothy Wright OSB in Kit Dollard, Anthony Marett-Crosby OSB, Abbot Timothy Wright OSB, *The Rule of St Benedict and Business Management: A Conversation* (London and New York: Continuum, 2002), pp. 128, 129.

8 Louis [Thomas] Merton OCSO, 'Monastic Vocation and Modern Thought', *Monastic Studies* 4 (Pine City, NY: Mount Saviour Monastery, 1966), p. 36.

9 *Desert Wisdom: Saying from the Desert Fathers*, trans. Yushi Nomura (Garden City NY: Doubleday & Co., 1982), p. 17.

10 Albert Holtz OSB, *Street Wisdom: Connecting with God in Everyday Life* (Mystic CT: Twenty-Third Publications, 2003), pp. 1–2.

11 A Carthusian, *The Spirit of Place: Carthusian Reflections* (London: Darton, Longman & Todd, 1998), p. 26.

12 Joan D. Chittister OSB, *Heart of Flesh: A Feminist Spirituality for Women and Men* (Grand Rapids MI and Cambridge, UK: Eerdmans, 1998), p. 142.

13 Michael Casey OCSO, *Strangers to the City: Reflections on the Beliefs and Values of the Rule of Saint Benedict* (Brewster MA: Paraclete Press, 2005), pp. 108–9.

14 *The Sayings of the Desert Fathers: The Alphabetical Collection*, trans. Benedicta Ward SLG (Kalamazoo MI: Cistercian Publications/Oxford: A. R. Mowbray, 1975, revised edn 1984), p. 89.

15 Sebastian Moore OSB, *The Fire and the Rose are One* (London: Darton, Longman & Todd, 1980), p. 64.

16 Laura Swan OSB, *Engaging Benedict: What the Rule Can Teach Us Today* (Notre Dame IN: Ave Maria Press, 2005), pp. 93–4.

17 Ciaran O'Sabhaois OCSO, from 'Community in the Early Irish Church', *Cistercian Studies* 10 (1975/1), pp. 64–5.

18 *The Wisdom of the Desert Fathers: Systematic Sayings from the Anonymous Series of the Apophthegmata Patrum*, trans. Benedicta Ward SLG (Oxford: SLG Press, 1986), no. 125.

19 Columba Stewart OSB, *Prayer and Community: The Benedictine Tradition* (London: Darton, Longman & Todd, 1998), p. 65.

20   Ciaran O'Sabhaois ocso, from 'Community in the Early Irish Church', *Cistercian Studies* 10 (1975/1), p. 65.

21   David Steindl-Rast osb, *A Listening Heart: The Art of Contemplative Living* (New York: Crossroad, 1983), pp. 78–9.

22   Kallistos Ware, footnote to 'The Spiritual Father in Orthodox Christianity', *Cross Currents* (Summer/Fall 1974), pp. 296–313.

23   Terence Kardong osb, from 'The Humanism of Benedict of Nursia' Part I, http://www.abcu.info/docs/kardonga.html (accessed 13/03/2006).

24   John Eudes Bamberger ocso, reported in Henri J. M. Nouwen, *The Genesee Diary: Report from a Trappist Monastery* (New York: Doubleday, 1989 [1981]), p. 48.

25   Columba Stewart osb, *Prayer and Community: The Benedictine Tradition* (London: Darton, Longman & Todd, 1998), p. 69.

26   Matthias Neuman osb, 'Modern Media and the Religious Sense of Community', *Review for Religious* 46/2 (March/April 1987), pp. 196 and 200–01.

27   Ruth Fox osb, 'Beyond Ecumenism: Religious as Pioneers', *Review for Religious* 54/1 (January/February 1995), p. 43.

28   André Louf ocso, *The Cistercian Alternative*, trans. Nivard Kinsella o cist (London: Gill & Macmillan, 1983), p. 129.

29   A Carthusian, *Poor, Therefore Rich: Carthusian Novice Conferences*, trans. an Anglican Solitary (London: Darton, Longman & Todd, 1999), pp. 107–8.

30   Donald W. Buggert o carm, from 'The Contemplative as Iconoclast: the Countercultural Nature of Contemplation', in *Carmel and Contemplation: Transforming Human Consciousness*, ed. Kevin Culligan ocd and Regis Jordan ocd (Washington DC: ICS Publications, 2000), p. 66.

31   Joan D. Chittister osb, *Twelve Steps to Inner Freedom: Humility Revisited* (Erie PA: Benetvision, 2003), pp. 80–1.

April

1   Armand Veilleux ocso, 'Called to Be Transformed into the Image of Christ (2 Cor. 3:18): Reflections on Monastic Formation', p. 6; first published in *A.I.M. Monastic Bulletin* 59 (1995). Revised Eng. trans. in http://users.skynet.be/scourmont/Armand/wri/formatio.htm (accessed 13/03/2006).

2   *The Wisdom of the Desert Fathers: Systematic Sayings from the Anonymous Series of the* Apophthegmata Patrum, trans. Benedicta Ward slg (Oxford: SLG Press, 1986), no. 115.

3   David Foster osb, *Reading with God: Lectio Divina* (London and New York: Continuum, 2005), p. v.

4   *Desert Wisdom: Sayings from the Desert Fathers*, trans. Yushi Nomura (Garden City NY: Doubleday & Co., 1982), p. 19.

5   Laurence Freeman osb, *Aspects of Love* (London and Berkhamsted: Medio Media/Arthur James, 1997), p. 10.

6   Joan Chittister OSB, 'Work: My Share of the Life of God', *Liguorian* (September 1993).

7   Benet Tvedten OSB, *How to Be a Monastic and not Leave your Day Job: An Invitation to Oblate Life* (Brewster MA: Paraclete Press, 2006), p. 16.

8   John Eudes Bamberger OCSO, as reported in Henri J. M. Nouwen, *The Genesee Diary: Report from a Trappist Monastery* (New York: Doubleday, 1989), p. 63.

9   Christopher Jamison OSB, 'The Benedictine Way', *The Tablet*, 20 May 2005, available at http://www.thetablet.co.uk (accessed 14/06/2006).

10   Timothy Wright OSB in Kit Dollard, Anthony Marett-Crosby OSB, Abbot Timothy Wright OSB, *The Rule of St Benedict and Business Management: A Conversation* (London and New York: Continuum, 2002), pp. 125–6.

11   From the *Life of Aelred* by Walter Daniel (monk of Rievaulx), ch 22, trans. Pauline Matarasso, *The Cistercian World: Writings in the Twelfth Century* (Harmondsworth: Penguin Books, 1993), p. 156.

12   *The Sayings of the Desert Fathers: The Alphabetical Collection*, trans. Benedicta Ward SLG (Kalamazoo MI: Cistercian Publications/Oxford: A. R. Mowbray, 1975, revised edn 1984), p. 75.

13   Michael Casey OCSO, *Sacred Writing: The Ancient Art of Lectio Divina* (Liguori MO: Liguori/Triumph, 1995), p. 8.

14   John Cassian, *Conferences* 14.6, trans. Colm Luibhead in *John Cassian: Conferences* (Mahwah NJ: Paulist Press, 1985), p. 158.

15   *The Desert Fathers: Sayings of the Early Christian Monks*, trans. Benedicta Ward SLG (London: Penguin Books, 2003), p. 66.

16   Columba Stewart OSB, *Prayer and Community: The Benedictine Tradition* (London: Darton, Longman & Todd, 1998), p. 65.

17   *The Desert Fathers: Sayings of the Early Christian Monks*, trans. Benedicta Ward SLG (London: Penguin Books, 2003), p. 63.

18   Archimandrite Sophrony, *His Life Is Mine*, trans. Rosemary Edmonds (London and Oxford: Mowbrays, 1977), p. 73.

19   Aelred Graham OSB, *Zen Catholicism* (New York: Crossroad/York: Ampleforth Abbey Press, 1963, 1994), p. 174.

20   Joan Chittister OSB, *Wisdom Distilled from the Daily: Living the Rule of St Benedict Today* (HarperSanFrancisco, 1991), p. 83.

21   Ruth Burrows, *To Believe in Jesus* (London: Sheed & Ward 1978), pp. 74–5.

22   Donald Corcoran OSB cam, in *The Privilege of Love: Camaldolese Benedictine Spirituality*, ed. Peter-Damian Belisle OSB cam (Collegeville MN: The Liturgical Press, 2002), p. 149.

23   John Climacus, *The Ladder of Divine Ascent*, trans. Colm Luibhead and Norman Russell (Mahwah NJ: Paulist Press/London: SPCK, 1982), p. 118.

24   Gregory the Great, *Be Friends of God: Spiritual Reading from Gregory the Great*, trans. John Leinenweber (Cambridge MA: Cowley Publications, 1990), p. 105.

25   *The Desert Fathers: Sayings of the Early Christian Monks*, trans. Benedicta Ward SLG (London: Penguin Books, 2003), p. 56.

26 Extract from the diary of Christophe Lebreton OCSO, translated and adapted by Martin McGee OSB, 'A Crucified Love: Extracts from the Diary of Fr Christophe of Tibirine', *Religious Life Review* Vol. 42 (July/August 2003), p. 195.

27 Joan Chittister OSB, *Wisdom Distilled from the Daily: Living the Rule of St Benedict Today* (HarperSanFrancisco, 1991), pp. 83–4.

28 John Climacus, *The Ladder of Divine Ascent*, trans. Colm Luibhead and Norman Russell (Mahwah NJ: Paulist Press/London: SPCK, 1982), p. 77.

29 John of the Cross, 'Sayings of Light and Love', no. 58, in *The Collected Works of St. John of the Cross*, trans. Kieran Kavanaugh OCD and Otilio Rodriguez OCD (Washington DC: Institute of Carmelite Studies Publications, 1979), p. 672.

30 Theophan the Recluse, from Letter 49, trans. Fr Stefan Pavlenko, *Orthodox Life* 32/4 (July/August 1982), pp. 21–30.

May

1 *Desert Wisdom: Sayings from the Desert Fathers*, trans. Yushi Nomura (New York: Doubleday & Company, Inc., 1982), pp. 42–3.

2 David Altman OCSO, 'The Values and Dangers of Fasting', *Review for Religious* 49/1 (January/February 1990), p. 125.

3 Joan Chittister OSB, *Wisdom Distilled from the Daily: Living the Rule of St Benedict Today* (HarperSanFrancisco, 1991), p. 78.

4 William McNamara OCD, *The Human Adventure: The Art of Contemplative Living* (Warwick NY: Amity House, 1974), p. 72.

5 Michael Casey OCSO, *Strangers to the City: Reflections on the Beliefs and Values of the Rule of Saint Benedict* (Brewster MA: Paraclete Press, 2005), p. 27.

6 Joan Chittister OSB, *Wisdom Distilled from the Daily: Living the Rule of St Benedict Today* (HarperSanFrancisco, 1991), p. 107.

7 André Louf OCSO, *The Cistercian Way* (Kalamazoo MI: Cistercian Publications, 1989), pp. 114–15.

8 Evagrius Ponticus in *Evagrius Ponticus – The Praktikos and Chapters on Prayer*, trans. John Eudes Bamberger OCSO (Spencer MA: Cistercian Publications, 1970).

9 Aelred of Rievaulx, Sermon 20, trans. A. Sulavik, 'Sermons on the feast of Saint Mary', *Cistercian Studies Quarterly* 32 (1997/1), pp. 51–2.

10 Paula Fairlie OSB, 'Foreshadowings' in Maria Boulding (ed.), *A Touch of God: Eight Monastic Journeys* (London: SPCK, 1982), p. 106.

11 Joan Chittister OSB, from an interview, 'Contemplation, Everyone?', published in *Praying Magazine* (January/February 1991).

12 Donald Corcoran OSB cam in *The Privilege of Love: Camaldolese Benedictine Spirituality*, ed. Peter-Damian Belisle (Collegeville MN: The Liturgical Press, 2002), p. 150.

13 Bede Griffiths OSB, *Selections from his Writings*, ed. Peter Spink (London: Darton, Longman & Todd, 1990).

14   Thomas Keating OCSO, *Invitation to Love* (New York: Crossroad, 1992).

15   *The Sayings of the Desert Fathers: The Alphabetical Collection*, trans. Benedicta Ward SLG (Kalamazoo MI: Cistercian Publications/Oxford: A. R. Mowbray, 1975, revised edn 1984), p. 234.

16   Michael Casey, *Sacred Writing: The Ancient Art of Lectio Divina* (Liguori MO: Liguori/Triumph, 1995), pp. 8–9.

17   Jeremy Driscoll OSB, *A Monk's Alphabet: Moments of Stillness in a Turning World* (London: Darton, Longman & Todd, 2006), pp. 64–5.

18   A Carthusian, *Where Silence Is Praise* (London: Darton, Longman & Todd, 1997), p. 5.

19   Frances Teresa OSC, *Living the Incarnation: Praying with Francis and Clare of Assisi* (London: Darton, Longman & Todd, 1993), pp. 59–60.

20   Albert Holtz OSB, *Street Wisdom: Connecting with God in Everyday Life* (Mystic CT: Twenty-Third Publications, 2003), pp. 40–1.

21   John Main OSB, *John Main: Arranged for Daily Reading*, comp. Clare Hallward (London: Darton, Longman & Todd, 1987; Springfield IL: Templegate Publishers, 1988), p. 87.

22   David Steindl-Rast OSB, *A Listening Heart: The Art of Contemplative Living* (New York: Crossroad, 1983), p. 21.

23   Aidan Byrne OCSO, *Monastic Studies* 2 (Berryville VA: Our Lady of the Holy Cross Abbey, 1964), p. 183.

24   Hildegard of Bingen, from a letter to an archbishop, trans. Ron Miller in Matthew Fox (ed.), *Hildegard of Bingen's Book of Divine Works, with Letters and Songs* (Santa Fe N. Mex.: Bear & Co., 1987), p. 283.

25   David Holly, 'Biblical Living', *Cistercian Studies* 10 (1975/1), p. 48 (slightly adapted).

26   Aelred Niespolo OSB, 'Healing Wounded Souls of Monk and Guest', *Religious Life Review* Vol. 43 (July/August 2004), p. 223.

27   Armand Veilleux OCSO, 'Called to Be Transformed into the Image of Christ (2 Cor. 3:18): Reflections on Monastic Formation', p. 3; first published in *A.I.M. Monastic Bulletin* 59 (1995). Revised Eng. trans. in http://users.skynet.be/scourmont/Armand/wri/formatio.htm (accessed 13/03/2006).

28   Amma Syncletica, from *The Life of Blessed Syncletica by Pseudo-Athanasius*, trans. Elizabeth Bryson Bongie (Toronto: Peregrina Publishing, 1995), p. 59.

29   Marie Beha OSC, 'Culture and Contemplative Community', *Review for Religious* 52/4 (July/August 1993), p. 592.

30   A Carthusian, *Poor, Therefore Rich: Carthusian Novice Conferences*, trans. an Anglican Solitary (London: Darton, Longman & Todd, 1999), p. 131.

31   Joan D. Chittister OSB, *Scarred by Struggle, Transformed by Hope* (Grand Rapids MI and Cambridge, UK: Eerdmans, 2003), p. 106.

June

1 Thomas Keating OCSO, *The Kingdom of God Is Like...* (New York: Crossroad, 1993), p. 47.

2 *Desert Wisdom: Saying from the Desert Fathers*, trans. Yushi Nomura (Garden City NY: Doubleday & Co., 1982), p. 47.

3 Joan Chittister OSB, *Wisdom Distilled from the Daily: Living the Rule of St Benedict Today* (HarperSanFrancisco, 1991), p. 164.

4 Frances Teresa OSC, *This Living Mirror: Reflections on Clare of Assisi* (London: Darton, Longman & Todd, 1995), p. 83.

5 *The Wisdom of the Desert Fathers: Systematic Sayings from the Anonymous Series of the* Apophthegmata Patrum, trans. Benedicta Ward SLG (Oxford: SLG Press, 1986), no. 126.

6 Michael Casey OCSO, *Strangers to the City: Reflections on the Beliefs and Values of the Rule of Saint Benedict* (Brewster MA: Paraclete Press, 2005), p. 77.

7 *The Wisdom of the Desert Fathers: Systematic Sayings from the Anonymous Series of the* Apophthegmata Patrum, trans. Benedicta Ward SLG (Oxford: SLG Press, 1986), no. 130.

8 John Cassian, *Conferences* 1.6, trans. Colm Luibheid in *John Cassian: Conferences* (Mahwah NJ: Paulist Press, 1985), p. 41.

9 *Letters from the Desert: Barsanuphius & John*, trans. John Chryssavgis (Crestwood NY: St Vladimir's Seminary Press, 2003), pp. 167–8.

10 Columba Stewart OSB, *Prayer and Community: The Benedictine Tradition* (London: Darton, Longman & Todd, 1998), p. 94.

11 *Letters from the Desert: Barsanuphius & John*, trans. John Chryssavgis (Crestwood NY: St Vladimir's Seminary Press, 2003), pp. 189–90.

12 André Louf OCSO, from *Mercy in Weakness: Meditations on the Word*, trans. John Vriend (London: Darton, Longman & Todd, 1998), pp. 28, 29 and 30.

13 *The Sayings of the Desert Fathers: The Alphabetical Collection*, trans. Benedicta Ward SLG (Kalamazoo MI: Cistercian Publications/Oxford: A. R. Mowbray, 1975, revised edn 1984), p. 172.

14 Bede Griffiths OSB, *Return to the Centre* (London: Collins, 1976), p. 12.

15 Maximus Confessor, from *The Four Hundred Chapters on Love*, Third Century 16–19, trans. George C. Berthold in *Maximus Confessor: Selected Writings* (Mahwah NJ: Paulist Press, 1985), p. 63.

16 *The Sayings of the Desert Fathers: The Alphabetical Collection*, trans. Benedicta Ward SLG (Kalamazoo MI: Cistercian Publications/Oxford: A. R. Mowbray, 1975, revised edn 1984), p. 24.

17 Thomas Merton, *Dancing in the Water of Life: The Journals of Thomas Merton, Vol. 5 1963–1965* (HarperSanFrancisco 1998), p. 98 (entry for April 21, 1964).

18 *The Wisdom of the Desert Fathers: Systematic Sayings from the Anonymous Series of the* Apophthegmata Patrum, trans. Benedicta Ward SLG (Oxford: SLG Press, 1986), p. 37.

19 A Carthusian, *Poor, Therefore Rich: Carthusian Novice Conferences*, trans. an Anglican Solitary (London: Darton, Longman & Todd, 1999), p. 172.

20 *Desert Wisdom: Sayings from the Desert Fathers*, trans. Yushi Nomura (New York: Doubleday & Company, Inc., 1982), p. 27.

21 Frances Teresa OSC, *Living the Incarnation: Praying with Francis and Clare of Assisi* (London: Darton, Longman & Todd, 1993), p. 78.

22 *The Sayings of the Desert Fathers: The Alphabetical Collection*, trans. Benedicta Ward, SLG (Kalamazoo MI: Cistercian Publications/Oxford: A. R. Mowbray, 1975, revised edn 1984), p. 242.

23 John Climacus, *The Ladder of Divine Ascent*, trans. Colm Luibhead and Norman Russell (Mahwah NJ: Paulist Press/London: SPCK, 1982), Step 17, p. 190.

24 Bede Griffiths OSB, *Return to the Centre* (London: Collins, 1976), p. 93.

25 *The Sayings of the Desert Fathers: The Alphabetical Collection*, trans. Benedicta Ward SLG (Kalamazoo MI: Cistercian Publications/Oxford: A. R. Mowbray, 1975, revised edn 1984), p. 233.

26 A Carthusian, *Poor, Therefore Rich: Carthusian Novice Conferences*, trans. an Anglican Solitary (London: Darton, Longman & Todd, 1999), pp. 172-3.

27 *The Sayings of the Desert Fathers: The Alphabetical Collection*, trans. Benedicta Ward SLG (Kalamazoo MI: Cistercian Publications/Oxford: A. R. Mowbray, 1975, revised edn 1984), p. 176.

28 *The Sayings of the Desert Fathers: The Alphabetical Collection*, trans. Benedicta Ward SLG (Kalamazoo MI: Cistercian Publications/Oxford: A. R. Mowbray, 1975, revised edn 1984), p. 73.

29 Joan Chittister OSB, *The Rule of Benedict: Insights for the Ages* (Slough: St Pauls, 1992), p. 108.

30 Constance Fitzgerald OCD, *Baltimore Carmel Newsletter* (September 2005) at http://www.baltimorecarmel.org (accessed 14/06/2006).

July

1 *The Wound of Love: A Carthusian Miscellany* (London: Darton, Longman & Todd, 1994), p. 45.

2 David Foster OSB, *Reading with God: Lectio Divina* (London and New York: Continuum, 2005), p. 4.

3 Roger Schutz, *Festival ...* (Taizé, France: Les Presses de Taizé, 1973), pp. 142-3.

4 Cyprian Consiglio OSB cam, in *The Privilege of Love: Camaldolese Benedictine Spirituality*, ed. Peter-Damian Belisle OSB cam (Collegeville MN: The Liturgical Press, 2004), p. 43.

5 James McCaffrey OCD, 'Focus', *Mt Carmel Magazine* 53/4 (October/December 2005). http://www.carmelite.org.uk/mteditorial.html (accessed 15/06/2006).

6 Aelred Niespolo OSB, 'Healing Wounded Souls of Monk and Guest', *Religious Life Review* 43 (July/August 2004), p. 219.

7 Basil the Great, from Letter 2 (Benedictine arrangement), trans. compilers.

8 Charles Cummings OCSO, *Monastic Practices*, Cistercian Studies Series 75 (Kalamazoo MI: Cistercian Publications, 1986), p. 96.

9 John Main OSB, *Letters from the Heart: Christian Monasticism and the Renewal of Community* (New York: Crossroad, 1988), p. 116.

10 David Steindl-Rast OSB, *A Listening Heart: The Art of Contemplative Living* (New York: Crossroad, 1983), pp. 9–10.

11 Joan D. Chittister OSB, *Scarred by Struggle, Transformed by Hope* (Grand Rapids MI: Eerdmans, 2003), p. 58.

12 Jeanne Ranek OSB, *American Monastic Newsletter* 35/3a (October 2005), Part 2. See http://www.osb.org/aba/news/2005/octa.html (accessed 04/04/2006).

13 Laura Swan OSB, from *The Forgotten Desert Mothers: Sayings, Lives and Stories of Early Christian Women* (New York/Mahwah NJ: Paulist Press, 2001), p. 159.

14 John Climacus, *The Ladder of Divine Ascent*, trans. Colm Luibhead and Norman Russell (Mahwah NJ: Paulist Press/London: SPCK, 1982), Step 11, pp. 158–9 (slightly adapted).

15 John Main OSB, *The Joy of Being*, selected by Clare Hallward (London: Darton, Longman & Todd, 1989), p. 37.

16 M. Basil Pennington OCSO, *The Cistercians* (Collegeville MN: The Liturgical Press, 1992), pp. 7–8.

17 Joan D. Chittister OSB, *Twelve Steps to Inner Freedom: Humility Revisited* (Erie PA: Benetvision, 2003), p. 67.

18 Peter-Damian Belisle OSB cam, *The Language of Silence: The Changing Face of Silence* (London: Darton, Longman & Todd, 2003), p. 18.

19 Pierre-François de Béthune OSB, *By Faith and Hospitality: The Monastic Tradition as a Model for Interreligious Encounter* (Leominster: Gracewing, 2002), pp. 5–6.

20 Marie Beha OSC, 'Becoming Contemplative: Here or There', *Review for Religious* 51/5 (September/October 1992), pp. 748–9.

21 Thomas Merton in a letter to Ernesto Cardenal (25 February 1963), in Thomas Merton, *The Courage for Truth: Letters to Writers*, ed. Christine M. Bochen (New York: Farrar, Straus, Giroux, 1993), p. 139.

22 *The Wisdom of the Desert Fathers: Systematic Sayings from the Anonymous Series of the* Apophthegmata Patrum, trans. Benedicta Ward SLG (Oxford: SLG Press, 1986), no. 105.

23 Christian de Chergé OCSO, from a conference given at the General Chapter of 1993 of his Order. http://www.ocso.org/xtian.htm (accessed 17/03/2006). Used by permission.

24 A Carthusian, *The Spirit of Place: Carthusian Reflections* (London: Darton, Longman & Todd, 1998), pp. 57, 59.

25 Michaela OSC, *A Little Book of Haiku*, p. 14 (available from the

Community of St Clare, St Mary's Convent, 178 Wroslyn Road, Freeland, Witney OX29 8AJ, UK).

26 Joan Chittister OSB, *Wisdom Distilled from the Daily: Living the Rule of St Benedict Today* (HarperSanFrancisco, 1991), p. 151.

27 Benedict Auer OSB, *Soulpoeting: Healing through Poetry* (London: St Pauls, 2000), pp. 31–2. Used by permission of St Pauls (formerly St Paul Publications), UK.

28 Michael Casey OCSO, *Sacred Writing: The Ancient Art of Lectio Divina* (Liguori MO: Liguori/Triumph, 1995), p. 89.

29 Thomas Merton in a letter to Ludovico Silva (10 April 1965), in Thomas Merton, *The Courage for Truth: Letters to Writers*, ed. Christine M. Bochen (New York: Farrar, Straus, Giroux, 1993), p. 225.

30 Peter-Damian Belisle OSB CAM, *The Language of Silence: The Changing Face of Silence* (London: Darton, Longman & Todd, 2003), pp. 19–20.

31 Fable found in the notes left by the Staretz Silouan, monk on Mt Athos, in *The Undistorted Image: Staretz Silouan: 1866–1938*, trans. Rosemary Edmonds (London: The Faith Press, 1958), pp. 94–5.

August

1 Laura Swan OSB, *Engaging Benedict: What the Rule Can Teach Us Today* (Notre Dame IN: Ave Maria Press, 2005), p. 143.

2 Ruth Burrows, *To Believe in Jesus* (London: Sheed and Ward, 1978), p. 68.

3 André Louf OCSO, *The Cistercian Way* (Kalamazoo MI: Cistercian Publications, 1989), pp. 60–1.

4 Joan D. Chittister OSB, *Heart of Flesh: A Feminist Spirituality for Women and Men* (Grand Rapids, MI, and Cambridge, UK: Eerdmans/Saint Paul University, Ottawa: Novalis, 1998), p. 1.

5 Christine Vladimiroff OSB, 'Blessing of ministries' at http://www.eriebenedictines.org/Pages/INSPIRATION/backprioress/blessingof ministries.html (accessed 10/04/2006).

6 Pierre-François de Béthune OSB, *By Faith and Hospitality: The Monastic Tradition as a Model for Interreligious Encounter* (Leominster: Gracewing, 2002), pp. 39–40.

7 Jeremy Driscoll OSB, *A Monk's Alphabet: Moments of Stillness in a Turning World* (London: Darton, Longman & Todd, 2006), pp. 6–7.

8 Joan Chittister OSB, 'Thomas Merton: Seeder of Radical Action and the Enlightened Heart', The Guilfoil Memorial Lecture, given in Kansas City MO, February 2001.

9 *Desert Wisdom: Sayings from the Desert Fathers*, trans. Yushi Nomura (Garden City NY: Doubleday & Co., 1982), p. 106.

10 Roger Schutz, *Festival ...* (Taizé, France: Les Presses de Taizé, 1973), pp. 37–8.

11 Isaac of Stella, *Sermons on the Christian Year Vol. 1*, trans. Hugh McCaffery (Kalamazoo MI: Cistercian Publications, 1979), p. 89.

12   Ramon Velasco OSB, 'Searching for God in Dialogue', Bulletin 70, March 2003, available at http://www.monasticdialog.com (accessed 14/06/2006).

13   Archimandrite Sophrony, *The Monk of Mount Athos* (London: A. R. Mowbray & Co., 1973), p. 32.

14   Frances Teresa OSC, *This Living Mirror: Reflections on Clare of Assisi* (London: Darton, Longman & Todd, 1995), p. 58.

15   *The Wisdom of the Desert Fathers: Systematic Sayings from the Anonymous Series of the* Apophthegmata Patrum, trans. Benedicta Ward SLG (Oxford: SLG Press, 1986), no. 224.

16   Benedictine Sisters, Monastery of St Gertrude, Cottonwood, Idaho. See http://stgertrudes.org/Ministry/Peace/peace.htm (accessed 15/06/2006).

17   Laura Swan OSB, *Engaging Benedict: What the Rule Can Teach Us Today* (Notre Dame IN: Ave Maria Press, 2005), p. 153.

18   Basil the Great, *The Long Rules – 1*, trans. M. Monica Wagner CSC (Boston MA: Daughters of St Paul, 1962), pp. 62–3.

19   From the Benedictine Peace Statement 2005. See http://www.stgertrudes.org/Ministry/Peace/peace_statement.htm (accessed 15/06/2006).

20   Joan D. Chittister OSB, *Scarred by Struggle, Transformed by Hope* (Grand Rapids MI and Cambridge, UK: Eerdmans, 2003), p. 80.

21   Bede Griffiths OSB in *The Universal Christ*, ed. Peter Spink (Darton, Longman & Todd 1993), p. 31.

22   Thomas Merton, *The Other Side of the Mountain: The Journals of Thomas Merton, Volume Seven 1967–1968*, ed. Patrick Hart OCSO (San Francisco: HarperSanFrancisco, 1999), p. 135.

23   Robert Hale OSB CAM, in *The Privilege of Love: Camaldolese Benedictine Spirituality*, ed. Peter-Damian Belisle OSB CAM (Collegeville MN: The Liturgical Press, 2002), pp. 109–10, quoting from Bruno-Boniface of Querfurt, *The Life of the Five Brothers*, trans. Thomas Matus, in *The Mystery of Romuald and the Five Brothers* (Big Sur CA: Source Books/Hermitage Books, 1994).

24   Vilma Seelaus OCD, from 'Teresa, Suffering, and the Face of God', in *Carmel and Contemplation: Transforming Human Consciousness*, ed. Kevin Culligan OCD and Regis Jordan OCD (Washington DC: ICS Publications, 2000), pp. 155–7.

25   Donald W. Buggert O CARM, from 'The Contemplative as Iconoclast: the Countercultural Nature of Contemplation', in *Carmel and Contemplation: Transforming Human Consciousness*, ed. Kevin Culligan OCD and Regis Jordan OCD (Washington DC: ICS Publications, 2000), pp. 65–6.

26   John of the Cross, 'Maxims on Love', no. 55, in *The Collected Works of St. John of the Cross*, trans. Kieran Kavanaugh OCD and Otilio Rodriguez OCD (Washington DC: ICS Publications, 1979), p. 678.

27   Armand Veilleux OCSO, 'Called to Be Transformed into the Image of Christ (2 Cor. 3:18): Reflections on Monastic Formation', pp. 2–3; first published in *A.I.M. Monastic Bulletin* 59 (1995). Revised Eng. trans. in http://users.skynet.be/scourmont/Armand/wri/formatio.htm (accessed 13/03/2006).

28   Pierre-François de Béthune OSB, *By Faith and Hospitality: The Monastic*

Tradition as a Model for Interreligious Encounter (Leominster: Gracewing, 2002), pp. 69–70.

29 Donald W. Buggert o carm, from 'The Contemplative as Iconoclast: the Countercultural Nature of Contemplation', in *Carmel and Contemplation: Transforming Human Consciousness*, ed. Kevin Culligan ocd and Regis Jordan ocd (Washington DC: ICS Publications, 2000), p. 67.

30 Gregory the Great, Homily 5 [Migne], trans. David Hurst in *Gregory the Great: Forty Gospel Homilies* (Kalamazoo MI: Cistercian Publications 1990), p. 12.

31 Bernardo Olivera ocso, Abbot General of the Cistercian Order, from 'Our Brothers of Atlas II', the account, sent to the houses of the Order, of his visit to Algeria after the kidnapping and death of seven Cistercian monks there in 1996. http://www.ocso.org/ag2-eng.htm (accessed 20/03/2006).

September

1 Bede Griffiths osb, *Essential Writings*, comp. Thomas Matus (Maryknoll NY: Orbis Books, 2004), p. 31.

2 Joan Chittister osb, 'Monastic Wisdom for Seekers of Light', *Religious Life Review* Vol. 40 (May/June 2001), p. 177.

3 William McNamara ocd, *The Human Adventure: The Art of Human Living* (Warwick NY: Amity House, 1974), p. 34.

4 John of the Cross, 'Maxims on Love', no. 79, in *The Collected Works of St. John of the Cross*, trans. Kieran Kavanaugh ocd and Otilio Rodriguez ocd (Washington DC: ICS Publications, 1979), p. 680.

5 Hubert van Zeller osb, *Leave Your Life Alone* (London: Sheed and Ward, 1973), p. 33.

6 Anthony Bloom, *Living Prayer* (London: Darton, Longman & Todd, 1966), p. 115.

7 André Louf ocso, from 'Spiritual Experience', *Cistercian Studies* 10 (1975/2), p. 133.

8 Marie Beha osc, 'Becoming Contemplative: Here or There', *Review for Religious* 51/5 (September/October 1992), pp. 744–5.

9 Bede Griffiths osb, *Selections from his Writings*, ed. Peter Spink (London: Darton, Longman & Todd, 1990).

10 Hubert van Zeller osb, *The Current of Spirituality* (Springfield IL: Templegate Publishers, 1970), pp. 64–5.

11 William McNamara ocd, *Mystical Passion: Spirituality for a Bored Society* (New York: Paulist Press, 1977), p. 56.

12 Jeremy Driscoll osb, *A Monk's Alphabet: Moments of Stillness in a Turning World* (London: Darton, Longman & Todd, 2006), p. 10.

13 Abhishiktananda (Henri le Saux osb), *Prayer* (London: SPCK, 1974), p. 6.

14 A Carthusian, *The Spirit of Place: Carthusian Reflections* (London: Darton, Longman & Todd, 1998), p. 34.

15 Aelred Graham OSB, *Zen Catholicism* (New York: Crossroad/York, UK: Ampleforth Abbey Press, 1994 [1963]), p. 159.

16 Gregory of Narek, *Lamentations of Narek: Mystic Soliloquies with God*, trans. Mischa Kudian (London: Mashtots Press, 1974, 1992).

17 Armand Veilleux OCSO, 'Called to Be Transformed into the Image of Christ (2 Cor. 3:18): Reflections on Monastic Formation', p. 5; first published in *A.I.M. Monastic Bulletin* 59 (1995). Revised Eng. trans. in http://users. skynet.be/scourmont/Armand/wri/formatio.htm (accessed 13/03/2006).

18 Evagrius Ponticus, no. 92 of 'The Hundred Chapters' in *Praktikos*, from *Praktikos, Chapters on Prayer*, trans. John Eudes Bamberger OCSO (Spencer MA: Cistercian Publications, 1970), p. 39.

19 Laura Swan OSB, *The Forgotten Desert Mothers: Sayings, Lives and Stories of Early Christian Women* (New York/Mahwah NJ: Paulist Press, 2001), p. 167.

20 Jeremy Driscoll OSB, *A Monk's Alphabet: Moments of Stillness in a Turning World* (London: Darton, Longman & Todd, 2006), p. 83.

21 Hilary Ottensmeyer OSB, 'The Problem with Problems', *Review for Religious* 54/5 (September/October 1995), p. 740.

22 Aelred Graham, *Zen Catholicism* (New York: Crossroad/York, UK: Ampleforth Abbey Press, 1994 [1963]), p. 141.

23 M. Basil Pennington OCSO, 'Monasticism: A Place of Deeper Unity', *Review for Religious* 48/4 (July/August 1989), pp. 537 and 540.

24 Joel Rippinger OSB, 'A Community of Contrasts: Reflections on Religious Life in the Third World', *Review for Religious* 48/1 (January/February 1989), pp. 83-4.

25 Anthony Bloom, *Courage to Pray*, trans. Dinah Livingstone (London: Darton, Longman & Todd/Crestwood NY: St Vladimir's Seminary Press, 1984), pp. 13-14.

26 John Eudes Bamberger OCSO, as reported in Henri J. M. Nouwen, *The Genesee Diary: Report from a Trappist Monastery* (New York: Doubleday, 1989), p. 119.

27 David Steindl-Rast OSB, *A Listening Heart: The Art of Contemplative Living* (New York: Crossroad, 1983), pp. 10-11.

28 Joan Chittister OSB, 'Metanoia: Call to Conversion', *Religious Life Review* Vol. 40 (July/August 2001), p. 244.

29 Charles Cummings OCSO, *Monastic Practices*, Cistercian Studies Series 75 (Kalamazoo MI: Cistercian Publications, 1986), pp. 138-9.

30 André Louf OCSO, *The Cistercian Way*, trans. Nivard Kinsella (Kalamazoo MI: Cistercian Publications, 1989), p. 57.

October

1 John of the Cross, 'Letters', no. 24, in *The Collected Works of St. John of the Cross*, trans. Kieran Kavanaugh OCD and Otilio Rodriguez OCD (Washington DC: ICS Publications, 1979), p. 703.

2   Bede Griffiths OSB, *Essential Writings*, comp. Thomas Matus (Maryknoll NY: Orbis Books, 2004), p. 115.

3   Thomas Keating OCSO, *The Human Condition: Contemplation and Transformation* (New York and Mahwah NJ: Paulist Press, 1999), pp. 21–2.

4   Charles Cummings OCSO, *Monastic Practices*, Cistercian Studies Series 75 (Kalamazoo MI: Cistercian Publications, 1986), pp. 147–8.

5   Laura Swan OSB, *The Forgotten Desert Mothers: Sayings, Lives and Stories of Early Christian Women* (New York/Mahwah NJ: Paulist Press, 2001), p. 165–6.

6   Christine Vladimiroff OSB, 'Lent is a time to model God's forgiveness in the world' at http://www.eriebenedictines.org/Pages/INSPIRATION/backprioress/lentvigil_04.html (accessed 10/04/2006).

7   Peter-Damian Belisle OSB CAM, *The Language of Silence: The Changing Face of Silence* (London: Darton, Longman & Todd, 2003), pp. 171–2.

8   Benedictine monks of New Camaldoli, from Bulletin 70, March 2003, available at http://www.monasticdialog.com (accessed 14/06/2006).

9   Basil Hume OSB, *To Be a Pilgrim: A Spiritual Notebook* (Slough: St Paul Publications, 1984), pp. 172–3.

10   The Monks of New Skete, *How to Be Your Dog's Best Friend: A Training Manual for Dog Owners* (Boston: Little, Brown & Co., 1978), pp. 191–2.

11   Thomas Merton, in an informal talk delivered at Calcutta, October 1968, published as Appendix II in *The Asian Journal of Thomas Merton* (London: Sheldon Press, 1974), pp. 305–6.

12   Charles Cummings OCSO, *Monastic Practices*, Cistercian Studies Series 75 (Kalamazoo MI: Cistercian Publications, 1986), p. 48.

13   Jeremy Driscoll OSB, *A Monk's Alphabet: Moments of Stillness in a Turning World* (London: Darton, Longman & Todd, 2006), p. 75.

14   Frances Teresa OSC, *Living the Incarnation: Praying with Francis and Clare of Assisi* (London: Darton, Longman & Todd, 1993), pp. 59–60.

15   A Carthusian, *The Spirit of Place: Carthusian Reflections* (London: Darton, Longman & Todd, 1998), p. 31.

16   John Main OSB, *Letters from the Heart: Christian Monasticism and the Renewal of Community* (New York: Crossroad, 1988), p. 70.

17   William MacNamara OCD, *The Human Adventure: The Art of Contemplative Living* (Warwick NY: Amity House, 1974), pp. 109–10.

18   Frances Teresa OSC, *Living the Incarnation: Praying with Francis and Clare of Assisi* (London: Darton, Longman & Todd, 1993), p. 90.

19   Donald Corcoran OSB CAM, in *The Privilege of Love: Camaldolese Benedictine Spirituality*, ed. Peter-Damian Belisle OSB CAM (Collegeville MN: The Liturgical Press, 2002), p. 154.

20   Vilma Seelaus OCD, 'Teresa, Suffering, and the Face of God', in *Carmel and Contemplation: Transforming Human Consciousness*, ed. Kevin Culligan OCD and Regis Jordan OCD (Washington DC: ICS Publications, 2000), pp. 139–40. The quoted passage is from Michael Talbot, *The Holographic Universe* (New York: Harper Perennial, 1992), p. 255.

21 Bede Griffiths OSB, *Essential Writings*, comp. Thomas Matus (Maryknoll NY: Orbis Books, 2004), pp. 96–7.

22 Ruth Fox OSB, 'Beyond Ecumenism: Religious as Pioneers', *Review for Religious* 54/1 (January/February 1995), pp. 42–3.

23 Staretz Silouan of Mount Athos, in Archimandrite Sophrony, *Wisdom from Mount Athos: The Writings of Staretz Silouan 1866–1938*, trans. Rosemary Edmonds (London: A. R. Mowbray, 1973).

24 Thomas Merton, in an informal talk delivered at Calcutta, October 1968, published as Appendix II in *The Asian Journal of Thomas Merton* (London: Sheldon Press, 1974), p. 306.

25 Joan D. Chittister OSB, *Heart of Flesh: A Feminist Spirituality for Women and Men* (Grand Rapids MI, and Cambridge, UK: Eerdmans/Saint Paul University, Ottawa: Novalis, 1998), p. 2.

26 Laura Swan OSB, *The Forgotten Desert Mothers: Sayings, Lives and Stories of Early Christian Women* (New York/Mahwah NJ: Paulist Press, 2001), p. 151.

27 Constance FitzGerald OCD, 'Impasse and Dark Night', in Tilden H. Edwards (ed.), *Living with Apocalypse: Spiritual Resources for Social Compassion* (New York: Harper & Row, 1984).

28 André Louf OCSO, *Teach Us to Pray: Learning a Little about God*, trans. Herbert Hoskins (London: Darton, Longman & Todd, 1974), pp. 19–20.

29 Christine Vladimiroff OSB, 'Blessing of ministries' at http://www.eriebenedictines.org/Pages/INSPIRATION/backprioress/blessingof ministries.html (accessed 10/04/2006).

30 Bruno Barnhart OSB CAM, in *The Privilege of Love: Camaldolese Benedictine Spirituality*, ed. Peter-Damian Belisle OSB CAM (Collegeville MN: The Liturgical Press, 2002), p. 76.

31 Joan Chittister OSB, *The Rule of Benedict: Insights for the Ages* (Slough: St Pauls, 1992), p. 55.

November

1 Basil Hume OSB, *In Praise of Benedict A.D. 480–1980* (London: Hodder & Stoughton, 1981), p. 36. From an address at Ealing Abbey, London, 21 March 1980.

2 David Steindl-Rast OSB, *Gratefulness, the Heart of Prayer: An Approach to Life in Fullness* (Ramsey NJ: Paulist Press, 1984), p. 17.

3 The Carthusian Order, The Renewed Statutes 28.4, quoted in A Carthusian, *Poor, Therefore Rich: Carthusian Novice Conferences*, trans. an Anglican Solitary (London: Darton, Longman & Todd, 1999), p. 184.

4 Virginia Cuthbert (V. M. Carver) CSCL, *The Great Shift: Life Seen as Sacramental* (Freeland, Oxfordshire: Community of St Clare, 1977), p. 53.

5 Bede, *A History of the English Church and People*, III.5, trans. Leo Sherley-Price (Harmondsworth: Penguin, 1955), p. 145.

6   Joan Chittister OSB, *The Rule of Benedict: Insights for the Ages* (Slough: St Pauls, 1992), pp. 108–9.

7   Hubert van Zeller OSB, *Leave Your Life Alone* (London: Sheed & Ward, 1973), p. 101.

8   Teresa of Avila, *The Way of Perfection*, ch. 28, trans. E. Allison Peers in *Complete Works of St Teresa* Vol. 2 (Sheed and Ward 1972), pp. 114–15.

9   Maria Boulding OSB, 'A Tapestry from the Wrong Side', in Maria Boulding (ed.), *A Touch of God: Eight Monastic Journeys* (London: SPCK, 1982), p. 43.

10   Christine Vladimiroff OSB, 'Reflections on the monastic life: Feast of Saint Scholastica' at http://www.eriebenedictines.org/Pages/INSPIRATION/backprioress/Scholastica.html (accessed 10/04/2006).

11   Benet Tvedten OSB, *How to Be a Monastic and not Leave your Day Job: An Invitation to Oblate Life* (Brewster MA: Paraclete Press, 2006), p. 49.

12   André Louf OCSO, *Tuning in to Grace: The Quest for God*, trans. John Vriend (London: Darton, Longman & Todd, 1992), p. 45.

13   Thomas Merton, in an informal talk delivered at Calcutta, October 1968, published as Appendix II in *The Asian Journal of Thomas Merton* (London: Sheldon Press, 1974), p. 307.

14   Pierre-François de Béthune OSB, *By Faith and Hospitality: The Monastic Tradition as a Model for Interreligious Encounter* (Leominster: Gracewing, 2002), pp. 5–6.

15   Joan Chittister OSB, 'Why I Stay', *Lutheran Woman Today*, October 1996.

16   Bede Griffiths OSB, *Selections from his Writings*, ed. Peter Spink (London: Darton, Longman & Todd, 1990).

17   David Steindl-Rast OSB, *Gratefulness, the Heart of Prayer: An Approach to Life in Fullness* (Ramsey NJ: Paulist Press, 1984), pp. 70–1.

18   *Letters from the Desert: Barsanuphius & John*, trans. John Chryssavgis (Crestwood NY: St Vladimir's Seminary Press, 2003), pp. 193–4.

19   Albert Holtz OSB, *Street Wisdom: Connecting with God in Everyday Life* (Mystic CT: Twenty-Third Publications, 2003), p. 36.

20   Frances Teresa OSC, *This Living Mirror: Reflections on Clare of Assisi* (London: Darton, Longman & Todd, 1995), p. 52.

21   *The Wisdom of the Desert Fathers: Systematic Sayings from the Anonymous Series of the Apophthegmata Patrum*, trans. Benedicta Ward SLG (Oxford: SLG Press, 1986), no. 150.

22   John Cassian, *Conferences* 2.6 (story told by the monk Moses), trans. Colm Luibhead in *John Cassian: Conferences* (Mahwah NJ: Paulist Press, 1985), pp. 65–6.

23   Aelred Graham OSB, *Zen Catholicism* (New York: Crossroad/York: Ampleforth Abbey Press, 1994 [1963]), p. 181.

24   Armand Veilleux OCSO, 'Benedictine Life as School of Communion' (1996) as found at http://users.skynet.be/scourmont/Armand/wri/koinonia.htm p. 4 (accessed 13/03/06).

25 Hilary Ottensmeyer OSB, 'Exegesis of Perversity Principles', *Review for Religious* 50/6 (November/December 1991), p. 927.
26 Suzanne Zuercher OSB, 'Monastic Parables', *Review for Religious* 48/6 (November/December 1989), p. 880. Used by permission.
27 David Steindl-Rast OSB, *Gratefulness, the Heart of Prayer: An Approach to Life in Fullness* (Ramsey NY: Paulist Press 1984), pp. 15–16.
28 André Louf OCSO, *Tuning in to Grace: The Quest for God*, trans. John Vriend (London: Darton, Longman & Todd, 1992), p. 113.
29 Joan D. Chittister OSB, *Scarred by Struggle, Transformed by Hope* (Grand Rapids MI and Cambridge, UK: Eerdmans, 2003), p. 69.
30 Elsie Felicity OSC, 'Spirituality and Ageing', *Franciscan* 10/3 (September 1998), p. 2.

December

1 Constance Fitzgerald, *Baltimore Carmel Newsletter* (September 2005) at http://www.baltimorecarmel.org (accessed 14/06/2006).
2 John of the Cross, 'Sayings of Light and Love', no. 53, in *The Collected Works of St. John of the Cross*, trans. Kieran Kavanaugh OCD and Otilio Rodriguez OCD (Washington DC: ICS Publications, 1979), p. 671.
3 Christopher Jamison OSB, *Finding Sanctuary: Monastic Steps for Everyday Life* (London: Weidenfeld and Nicolson, 2006), p. 172.
4 Michael Casey OCSO, *Strangers to the City: Reflections on the Beliefs and Values of the Rule of Saint Benedict* (Brewster MA: Paraclete Press, 2005), p. 197.
5 David Steindl-Rast OSB, *Gratefulness, the Heart of Prayer: An Approach to Life in Fullness* (Ramsey NJ: Paulist Press, 1984), p. 126.
6 John Main OSB, in *The Joy of Being*, ed. Clare Hallward (London: Darton, Longman & Todd, 1989), p. 19.
7 Neilos the Ascetic, *Ascetic* Discourse in *The Philokalia* Vol. 1, trans. G. E. H. Palmer, Philip Sherrard and Kallistos Ware (London: Faber & Faber 1979), pp. 236–7.
8 Leonard Vickers OSB, 'On a Human Note' in Maria Boulding OSB (ed.), *A Touch of God: Eight Monastic Journeys* (London: SPCK, 1982), pp. 120–1.
9 David Morland OSB, 'A Spiritual Jigsaw' in Maria Boulding OSB (ed.), *A Touch of God: Eight Monastic Journeys* (London: SPCK, 1982), p. 90.
10 Thomas Merton, *The Courage for Truth: Letters to Writers*, ed. Christine M. Bochen (New York: Farrar, Straus, Giroux, 1993), p. 29 (letter to Jacques Maritain 22 February 1960).
11 Jeremy Driscoll OSB, *A Monk's Alphabet: Moments of Stillness in a Turning World* (London: Darton, Longman & Todd, 2006), pp. 4–5.
12 Teresa of Avila, *Soliloquy* 17.6 in *The Collected Works of St. Teresa of Avila*, Vol. 1, trans. Kieran Kavanagh OCD and Otilio Rodriguez OCD (Washington DC: ICS Publications, 1987).
13 Frances Teresa OSC, *This Living Mirror: Reflections on Clare of Assisi* (London: Darton, Longman & Todd, 1995), pp. 56–7.

14 Joan D. Chittister OSB, *Scarred by Struggle, Transformed by Hope* (Grand Rapids MI/Cambridge, UK: Eerdmans, 2003), p. 54.

15 *Desert Wisdom: Sayings from the Desert Fathers*, trans. Yushi Nomura (Garden City NY: Doubleday & Co., 1982), p. 90.

16 Sister Frances Teresa OSC, *Living the Incarnation: Praying with Francis and Clare of Assisi* (London: Darton, Longman & Todd, 1993), p. 9.

17 Christophe Lebreton OSCO, quoted in a letter of the Abbot General of his Order, following his murder, with six of his fellow monks, in Algeria in 1996. http://www.ocso.org/ag2-eng.htm (accessed 20/03/06). Used by permission.

18 Christian de Chergé OCSO, 'TESTAMENT' at http://www.ocso.org/testc-vv.htm (accessed 20/03/06). Used by permission.

19 Joan Chittister OSB, 'When Numbers Don't Count', *Religious Life Review* Vol. 38 (January/February 1999), p. 7.

20 Matthias Neuman OSB, 'Newman's Living the Oratory Charism', *Review for Religious* 51/2 (March/April 1992), p. 223, quoting from J. H. Newman, *The Dream of Gerontius*.

21 Marie Beha OSC, 'In the Valley of Decision', *Review for Religious* 50/2 (March/April 1991), p. 202.

22 Laura Swan OSB, *The Forgotten Desert Mothers: Sayings, Lives and Stories of Early Christian Women* (New York/Mahwah NJ: Paulist Press, 2001), p. 155.

23 Basil Pennington OCSO, *Who Do You Say That I Am? Meditations on Jesus' Questions in the Gospels* (Hyde Park NY: New City Press, 1999), p. 13.

24 Gregory the Great, from homily 8 on the Gospel, intended for Christmas Day, trans. Aelred Squire, in *Fathers Talking: An Anthology* (Kalamazoo MI: Cistercian Publications, 1986), p. 14.

25 Thomas Merton, a special closing prayer, offered at the First Spiritual Summit Conference in Calcutta (1968), published as Appendix V in *The Asian Journal of Thomas Merton* (London: Sheldon Press, 1974), pp. 318–19.

26 *The Wisdom of the Desert Fathers: Systematic Sayings from the Anonymous Series of the* Apophthegmata Patrum, trans. Benedicta Ward SLG (Oxford: SLG Press, 1986), no. 147.

27 André Louf OCSO, *Tuning in to Grace: The Quest for God*, trans. John Vriend (London: Darton, Longman & Todd, 1992), p. 6.

28 Anthony Bloom, in Metropolitan Anthony and Georges Lefebvre OSB, *Courage to Pray*, trans. Dinah Livingstone (London: Darton, Longman & Todd/Crestwood NY: St Vladimir's Seminary Press, 1984), pp. 12–13.

29 Abhishiktananda (Henri le Saux OSB), *Guru and Disciple*, trans. Heather Sandeman (London: SPCK, 1974), pp. 150–1.

30 Isaac of Stella, *Sermons on the Christian Year Vol. 1*, trans. Hugh McCaffery (Kalamazoo MI: Cistercian Publications, 1979), p. 209.

31 Thomas Merton, *The Other Side of the Mountain: The Journals of Thomas Merton, Volume Seven 1967–1968*, ed. Patrick Hart OCSO (San Francisco: HarperSanFrancisco, 1999), p. 113.

Biographical index

Abhishiktananda (Henri le Saux OSB, 1910–73) was a French Benedictine who lived in a hermitage at Gyansu in the Himalayas, near the source of the Ganges.
Feb. 2; Sept. 13; Dec. 29

Aelred of Rievaulx (1109–67) was an English monk.
Feb. 16; Mar. 5; May 9

Abba Agathon (d. 370) was one of the Desert Fathers.
June 16

David Altman OCSO is a monk of Holy Trinity Abbey, Huntsville, Utah.
May 2

Abba Ammonas was one of the Desert Fathers.
Feb. 24

Anselm of Canterbury (1033–1109) was a monk of the monastery of Bec in Normandy (and later Archbishop of Canterbury).
Jan. 31

Antony the Great (c. 251–356) was one of the earliest Desert Fathers.
Feb. 20, 28

Benedict Auer OSB is a member of St Martin's Monastic Community, Lacey, WA.
Jan. 7; July 27

John Eudes Bamberger OCSO, monk of Genesee, New York State.
Mar. 24; Apr. 8; Sept. 26

Bruno Barnhart OSB CAM, monk of New Camaldoli Hermitage, Big Sur, California.
Oct. 30

Basil of Caesarea (Basil the Great; 330–379) lived for a time as an ascetic, with others, in Annisa (present-day Turkey).
Jan. 4; Feb. Rule; Mar. Rule; July 7; Aug. 18; Sept. Rule; Nov. Rule

Benedictine monks of New Camaldoli, Big Sur, California.
Oct. 8

Benedictine Sisters, Monastery of St Gertrude, Idaho, USA.
Aug. 16

Bede (673–735), an English monk of the monastery at Jarrow, Northumbria.
Nov. 5

Marie Beha OSC is a Poor Clare of Greenville, South Carolina, USA.
Jan. 19, 27; May 29; July 20; Sept. 8; Dec. 21

Peter-Damian Belisle OSB CAM, monk of New Camaldoli Hermitage, Big Sur, California.
July 18, 30; Oct. 7

Benedict of Nursia (c. 480–543), Italian father of the Benedictine Order.
Jan. Rule; Apr. Rule; May Rule; June Rule; July Rule; Aug. Rule; Oct. Rule; Dec. Rule

Anthony Bloom (1914–2003) was a monk of the Russian Orthodox Church.
Jan. 15; Feb. 21; Sept. 6, 25; Dec. 28

Aquinata Böckmann OSB is a member of the Benedictine Missionary Sisters of Tutzing, Germany.
Jan. 1; Feb. 15

Maria Boulding OSB is a Benedictine nun of Stanbrook Abbey, England.
Nov. 9

Donald W. Buggert O CARM is a Carmelite friar resident at Whitefriars Hall, Washington Theological Union, Washington DC.
Mar. 30; Aug. 25, 29

Ruth Burrows is an English Carmelite.
Feb. 8; Apr. 21; Aug. 2

Aidan Byrne OCSO, monk of Caldey Abbey, Wales.
May 23

A Carthusian (anonymous writings by members of the Carthusian Order).
Jan. 14; Mar. 11, 29; May 18, 30; June 19, 26; July 1, 24; Sept. 14; Oct. 15; Nov. 3

Michael Casey OCSO is a Cistercian monk of Tarrawarra Abbey in Australia.
Feb. 4, 11; Mar. 13; Apr. 13, May 5, 16; June 6; July 28; Dec. 4

John Cassian (c. 360–c. 435) was a monk of southern Gaul.
Apr. 14; June 8; Nov. 22

Joan Chittister OSB is a member of the community of Benedictine Sisters of Erie, USA.
Jan. 9, 30; Feb. 9, 22, 29; Mar, 2, 12, 31; Apr. 6, 20, 27; May 3, 6, 11, 31; June 3, 29; July 11, 17, 26; Aug. 4, 8, 20; Sept. 2, 28; Oct. 25, 31; Nov. 6, 15, 29; Dec. 14, 19

Jean Chively OSC, Poor Clare of Greenville, South Carolina.
Jan. 17

A Cistercian monk, an unnamed 'unstable brother' of Rievaulx in the time of Aelred.
Apr. 11

Cyprian Consiglio OSB CAM, monk of New Camaldoli Hermitage, Big Sur, California.
July 4

Donald Corcoran OSB Cam., nun of Transfiguration Monastery, Windsor, New York.

Apr. 22; May 12; Oct. 19

Charles Cummings OCSO is a Cistercian monk.

July 8; Sept. 29; Oct. 4, 12

Pierre-François de Béthune OSB is a monk of the Monastery of Clerlande, Belgium.

July 19; Aug. 6, 28; Nov. 14

Christian de Chergé OCSO was a monk of the Cistercian monastery at Tibhirine (Atlas) in Algeria, murdered with six other Cistercians in 1996.

July 23; Dec. 18

Jeremy Driscoll OSB is a Benedictine monk whose monastery is in Oregon, USA.

May 17; Aug. 7; Sept. 12, 20; Oct. 13; Dec. 11

Elsie Felicity OSC (1917–2006) was a member of the Community of St Clare at Freeland, UK.

Nov. 30

Evagrius Ponticus (c. 345–399), monk and hermit of the desert.

Feb. 27; May 8; Sept. 18

Paula Fairlie OSB, Benedictine nun of Stanbrook Abbey, UK.

May 10

Constance FitzGerald OCD is a Carmelite nun at the Baltimore Carmel, USA.

June 30; Oct. 27; Dec. 1

David Foster OSB is a Benedictine monk of Downside Abbey, UK.

Apr. 3; July 2

Ruth Fox OSB is a member of the community at Sacred Heart Monastery, Richardson, North Dakota.

Mar. 27; Oct. 22

Frances Teresa OSC is an English Poor Clare.

Feb. 7; May 19; June 4, 21; Aug. 14; Oct. 14, 18; Nov. 20; Dec. 13, 16

Laurence Freeman OSB is a Benedictine monk of the Monastery of Christ the King, Cockfosters, London.

Apr. 5

Aelred Graham OSB was a monk of Ampleforth Abbey, Yorkshire, UK.

Apr. 19; Sept. 15, 22; Nov. 23

Gregory of Narek (951–1003) was a monk of the Armenian Church.

Sept. 16

Gregory the Great (540–604) was an Italian monk (later Pope).

Jan. 29; Apr. 24; Aug. 30; Dec. 24

Bede Griffiths OSB was an English Benedictine monk who settled in India in 1955, where he established a Christian community following the customs of a Hindu ashram.

May 13; June 14, 24; Aug. 21; Sept. 1, 9; Oct. 2, 21; Nov. 16

Robert Hale OSB CAM, monk of New Camaldoli Hermitage, Big Sur, California.

    Aug. 23

Hildegard of Bingen (1098–1179) was a Benedictine nun.

    May 24

David Holly OCSO is a Cistercian monk based in Rome.

    May 25

Albert Holtz OSB is a Benedictine monk of Newark Abbey, USA.

    Jan. 25; Feb. 25; Mar. 10; May 20; Nov. 19

Basil Hume OSB (1923–99) was a Benedictine monk of Ampleforth Abbey, England.

    Jan. 11; Oct. 9; Nov. 1

Abba Isidore was one of the Desert Fathers.

    Apr. 17

Abba James was one of the Desert Fathers.

    Aug. 9

Christopher Jamison OSB is a Benedictine monk of Worth Abbey, UK.

    Apr. 9; Dec. 3

Abba John was one of the Desert Fathers.

    Mar. 14

John, a sixth-century monk who lived around Gaza.

    June 9, 11; Nov. 18

John of the Cross (1542–91) was, with Teresa of Avila, a founder of the Discalced Carmelites and lived in Spain.

    Apr. 29; Aug. 26; Sept. 4; Oct. 1; Dec. 2

John Climacus (c. 570–649) was a monk on Mount Sinai.

    Jan. 28; Apr. 23, 28; June 23; July 14

Abba Joseph was one of the Desert Fathers.

    Dec. 15

Terrence Kardong OSB is a Benedictine monk of Assumption Abbey, Richardton, North Dakota.

    Mar. 23

Thomas Keating OCSO, former abbot of St Joseph's Abbey in Spencer, Massachusetts.

    Jan. 10, 16; May 14; June 1; Oct. 3

Christophe Lebreton OCSO was a monk at Tibhirine (Atlas) in Algeria, murdered with six other Cistercians in 1996.

    Apr. 26; Dec. 17

Jean Leclercq OSB (d. 1993) was a Benedictine monk of Clervaux Abbey, Luxembourg.

    Jan. 6

André Louf ocso, monk of the Cistercian Abbey of Sainte-Marie-du-Mont, known also as Mont des Cats.

Jan. 8, 21; Mar. 6, 28; May 7; June 12; Aug. 3; Sept. 7, 30; Oct. 28; Nov. 12, 28; Dec. 27

Macarius the Great (Macarius of Egypt; *c.* 300–*c.*390) was one of the Desert Fathers.

Feb. 5

John Main osb (1926–82) was an English Benedictine monk.

Jan. 12, 18; Feb. 19; May 21; July 9, 15; Oct. 16; Dec. 6, 12

Maximus Confessor (580–662) was a Greek monk of the Orthodox Church.

June 15

James McCaffrey ocd, Carmelite friar in Oxford, England.

Feb. 13; July 5

William McNamara ocd is a Discalced Carmelite.

Jan. 26; May 4; Sept. 3, 11; Oct. 17

Thomas (Louis) Merton (1915–68) was a monk of the Cistercian Order of Strict Observance at the Abbey of Gethsemani, Kentucky, USA.

Mar. 8; June 17; July 21, 29; Aug. 22; Oct. 11, 24; Nov. 13; Dec. 10, 25, 31

Michaela osc is a member of the Community of St Clare at Freeland, UK.

July 25

Monks of New Skete, members of an Orthodox monastery in the hills outside Cambridge, New York.

Oct. 10

Sebastian Moore osb is an English Benedictine monk of Downside Abbey.

Mar. 15

David Morland osb, English Benedictine monk of Ampleforth Abbey.

Dec. 9

Abba Moses (d. *c.* 375) was one of the Desert Fathers.

Nov. 22

Neilos the Ascetic (d. *c.* 430) was one of the Desert Fathers.

Dec. 7

Abba Nesteros was one of the Desert Fathers.

Apr. 14

Matthias Neuman osb is a monk of St Meinrad Archabbey, Indiana.

Mar. 26; Dec. 20

Aelred Niespolo osb is a monk of St Andrew's Abbey, Valyermo, California.

May 26; July 6

Bernardo Olivera ocso is Abbot General of the Cistercian Order.

Aug. 31

Ciaran O'Sabhaois is an Irish Cistercian monk.

Mar. 17, 20

Hilary Ottensmeyer osb (1923–2000) was a monk of St Meinrad Archabbey, Indiana.

Sept. 21; Nov. 25

M. Basil Pennington OCSO (1931–2005) was a Cistercian monk of St Joseph Abbey, Spencer, Massachusetts.

Jan. 2; Feb. 26; July 16; Sept. 23; Dec. 23

Abba Philagrius was one of the Desert Fathers.

June 22

Abba Pistamon was one of the Desert Fathers.

Apr. 25

Abba Poemen (d. *c.* 449) was one of the Desert Fathers.

Jan. 5

Jeanne Ranek OSB is a member of the Benedictine community of Sacred Heart Monastery, Yankton, South Dakota.

July 12

Joel Rippinger OSB, a monk of the community at Priorato de San Jose, Solola, Guatemala.

Sept. 24

Romuald of Ravenna (*c.* 950–1027), the founder of the original Camaldolese monastery.

Jan. 13

Roger Schutz (Brother Roger; 1915–2005) was the founder of the ecumenical Taizé community in France.

July 3; Aug. 10

Vilma Seelaus OCD is a member of the Carmelite community in Barrington, Rhode Island.

Aug. 24; Oct. 20

Seraphim of Sarov (1759–1833) was a monk of the Russian Orthodox Church.

Feb. 23

Staretz Silouan (1866–1938) was a Russian monk of Mount Athos, Greece.

July 31

Archimandrite Sophrony (Sakharov) (1896–1993) was a Russian monk of Mount Athos who later founded a monastery in the UK.

Feb. 6; Apr. 18; Aug. 13; Oct. 23

Kurt Stasiak OSB is a Benedictine monk of St Meinrad Archabbey, Indiana.

Jan. 24

David Steindl-Rast OSB is a Benedictine monk of the monastery of Mount Saviour in Elmira, New York.

Mar. 21; May 22; July 10; Sept. 27; Nov. 2, 17, 27; Dec. 5

Columba Stewart OSB is a Benedictine monk of St John's Abbey, Collegeville, Minnesota.

Feb. 17; Mar. 19, 25; Apr. 16; June 10

Laura Swan OSB is a Benedictine nun of St Placid Priory, in the Pacific Northwest (USA).

Jan. 3, 20; Feb. 1; Mar. 16; July 13; Aug. 1, 17; Sept. 19; Oct. 5, 26; Dec. 22

Abba Sylvanus was one of the Desert Fathers.
   May 1
Amma Syncletica (380–c. 460) was one of the Desert Mothers.
   Apr. 4; May 15, 28; June 25

Teresa of Avila (1515–82) was a Spanish Carmelite reformer and mystic.
   Nov. 8; Dec. 12
Amma Theodora was one of the Desert Mothers.
   Feb. 14
Abba Theodore was one of the Desert Fathers.
   Apr. 12; June 28
Theophan the Recluse (1815–1894) was a monk of the Russian Orthodox Church.
   Apr. 30
Benet Tvedten OSB is a Benedictine monk of Blue Cloud Abbey, South Dakota, USA.
   Apr. 7; Nov. 11

Hubert van Zeller OSB (1905–84) was an English Benedictine monk of Downside Abbey.
   Sept. 5, 10; Nov. 7
Armand Veilleux OCSO, Cistercian monk of Scourmont Abbey in Belgium.
   Apr. 1; May 27; Aug. 27; Sept. 17; Nov. 24
Ramon Velasco OSB is a Benedictine monk living at Santo Domingo de Silos in Spain.
   Aug. 12
Leonard Vickers OSB is an English Benedictine monk of Douai Abbey.
   Dec. 8
Virginia Cuthbert (V. M. Carver) CSCL was a member of the Community of St Clare at Freeland, UK.
   Nov. 4
Christine Vladimiroff OSB is a member of the Benedictine Sisters of Erie, USA.
   Mar. 4; Aug. 5; Oct. 6, 29; Nov. 10

Kallistos Ware is a monk of the Monastery of St John, Patmos (Greece), living in Oxford, UK.
   Feb. 3; Mar. 22
Timothy Wright OSB is Abbot of Ampleforth, the Benedictine monastery in Yorkshire, UK.
   Jan. 22, 23; Mar. 7; Apr. 10

Suzanne Zuercher OSB is a member of the Benedictine Sisters of St Scholastica Priory in Chicago.
   Nov. 26